JN241767

Critical Reading through Collaborative Learning

舘岡洋子 監修
津田ひろみ・大須賀直子・小松千明・Alison Stewart 著

ひつじ書房

目次

はじめに 1

GETTING STARTED **Wake up!** 7

UNIT ONE **Nurture & Nature** 11

Reading 1 In Cross-Cultural Situations, Remember Those Emoticons — 13

Reading 2 Nurture as Important as Nature for Success — 19

Reading 3 It Begins at 10: How Gender Expectations Shape Early Adolescence Around the World — 25

UNIT TWO **Group & Individual** 33

Reading 1 The Secret to Smart Groups: It's Women — 35

Reading 2 Japanese Firms Need More Diverse Workforce, Says Harvard Academic — 43

Reading 3 The Power of Introverts: A Manifesto for Quiet Brilliance — 50

UNIT THREE **Language & Communication** 59

Reading 1 A Linguistic Big Bang — 61

Reading 2 Could the Lingua Franca Approach to Learning Break Japan's English Curse? — 70

Reading 3 Love That Lingua Franca. Trip Talk: Travel Encounters Can Benefit From a Common Third Language — 78

UNIT FOUR **Learning & Emotion** 87

Reading 1 To Help Students Learn, Engage the Emotion — 89

Reading 2 The Effort Effect — 96

Reading 3 The Dark Side of Emotional Intelligence — 103

APPENDIX **Useful Phrases and Vocabulary for Effective Writing** 114

WEBSITES 117

はじめに

Franzi/Shutterstock

今、この本を手にとっていらっしゃる皆さんは、たぶん英語を勉強中の方々だろうと思います。そんな皆さんに、唐突ですが質問です。皆さんは、なぜ英語を勉強しているのですか。大学の卒業に必要な単位を取るためですか。資格試験で高得点を取ろうと頑張っているのですか。それとも、留学のための準備でしょうか。あるいは、就職のために英語力を高めようとしているのかもしれません。いずれも重要な目的にちがいありませんが、本書はそうした英語力の向上だけに留まらず、さまざまな英文を手がかりに社会や自分を見つめ直し、異なる考えを持つ仲間たちと意見交換をしながら自分自身の考えを深めていく、そうした協働的な学びをめざしているのです。

■ 協働学習

このリーディングテキストは日本語教育のための『協働で学ぶクリティカル・リーディング』(2015年、舘岡洋子編著、ひつじ書房)[1]の英語版 として企画されました。

intermediate ~ advanced レベルの大学生の皆さんを対象に、協働学習を基本として組み立てられています。まず、協働学習とは一体何でしょうか？　一言で言うならば、それは学習者主体の授業形態です。つまり、教師が前に立って教えるのではなく、学生の皆さんがお互いに意見を交換し学び合いながら理解を深めていくやり方です。その協働学習は、単なる知識の獲得、たとえば単語の意味を答えるとか文法上正しい語法を選ぶといった正解がひとつに決まっている学習にはあまり向きません。協働学習にふさわしいのは、学生の皆さんが一人ひとり異なる考えをもつことが求められ、お互いの考えを聞き合って、さらに自分の考えを深めることができるような場面です。だからといって、一人ひとりがばらばらに自分の意見を表明し、それだけで終わってしまっては協働学習の本当の効果は期待できません。話し合い（学習の場における相互行為）を通して各自が何かを感じ取り、そこからもう一度自分自身を振り返ることが必要です。言い換えれば、協働学習では一人ひとりが責任をもって自分の役割（個人の学習）を果たした上で、いろいろな考えを受け入れること（多様性の受容）が求められるのです。「受け入れる」というのは鵜呑みにするということではありません。よく耳を傾け、理解した上で自分の考えと照らし合わせ、どこが共通してどこが異なるのか、どう異なるのか、なぜ異なるのか、よく考えることです。そのためには仲間とじっくり話し合う必要があります。このように、協働学習は決して単なるグループ学習ではないことを忘れないでください。

■ テキストの４つのテーマ

英語は今や global language (Lingua Franca) であり、英語を学ぶことは global citizenship を備えた自分を形作るプロセスとも言えます。このテキストは、学生の皆さんに深く考えてほしい４つのテーマについて、様々な視点から書かれた英語のパッセージを集めたものです。まず、英語で書かれたパッセージを読んで論理的な思考の進め方を学んでください。次に、書かれている内容をしっかり理解してください。英語を英語で読んで理解し、英語で話し合い、英語で考えることにぜひ挑戦してください！

■ テキストがめざすもの

このテキストの目的は次の 3 点で、そのうち 2) と 3) が従来の reading のテキストと異なる特徴だろうと思います。

1) ある程度まとまりのある英語の文章を読むことの愉しさを味わい、要点を掴みながら読むことに慣れる
2) その内容について批判的・論理的に思考する力を鍛える
3) 話し合いを通して自分を取り巻く社会（他者）を知り、同時に自分自身を客観的にみつ

める力をつける

■ テキストの構成

このような目的をもって準備されたテキストの構成と概要は以下のとおりです。

まず、テキストは4つのユニットから構成されており、各ユニットにはテーマがあります。そのテーマに沿って3つのパッセージが並んでいます。どのパッセージもオンラインのジャーナルから選ばれたauthenticな読み物です。(ただし、長いパッセージは一部を抜粋したり、省略したりしています。) もし、その中に固有名詞やアメリカの文化など耳慣れないものがあったなら、インターネットなどを活用して積極的に調べてください。4つのユニットは先に進むにつれテーマも英語の文章も少しずつ難しくなっていきます。そして、各パッセージには協働学習を進めるための8つのステップが準備されています。どこかのステップで躓いたら、そのときはStep 2 [Reading] に戻ってください。各ユニットの終わりにはOptionのexerciseがありますので、余裕があれば、ぜひ楽しんでチャレンジしてみてください。

Step 1【準備】Warm-up (Pre-reading Questions, Vocabulary Check)
　問いと語彙学習によってテーマに関する予備知識を喚起する
Step 2【読み】Reading　さあ、読んでみましょう
Step 3【理解】Understanding the Reading　内容に関する理解問題
Step 4【確認】Getting the Main Idea　自分の理解を仲間と共に確認する
Step 5【自分】Personalizing　自分の問題として考える (メモを取る)
Step 6【聞く】Sharing　他の人の意見と共通する点や異なる点に気づく
Step 7【思考】Critical Thinking & Reflection　他の人の考えを聞いて省察する
Step 8【発信】Expressing Your Ideas　各パッセージのテーマについて自分の意見をまとめ
　仲間に向けて発信する
Option【発表】Unit End Tasks
　1) Opinion Writing　各ユニットのテーマについて自分の意見をまとめる
　2) Group Project　グループ・プレゼンテーションをする

■ 学びの3つの出会いと対話

教育学の専門家である佐藤学氏は、その著書『学校の挑戦：学びの共同体を創る』(2006, 小学館) [2] の中で、学びの「内化」には3つの出会いと対話が必要であると述べています。まず、対象 (教材) である新しい世界との出会いと対話、次に、他者 (仲間や教師) との出会いと対話、そして最後に自己との出会いと対話、この3つの段階を経ながら次第に理

解を深めるというのです。そして、協働学習はこれら3つの出会いを実現することができるため、学びを深めるのに有効であるといいます。皆さんもこのテキストを通して3つの出会いと対話を経験しながら、各パッセージと取り組んでいただきたいと思います。そのために、パッセージに向き合うときには「自分はどう考える？」という主体的な視点をもつことを忘れないでください。つねに自分に問いかけながら読みすすめていくと、「おやっ」と思うところがきっと出てくるでしょう。そのことについて、今度は仲間の意見や考えを聞いてみてください。自分には思いもよらない考えが聞けるかもしれません。それをきっかけにして、もう一度あなた自身に問い、あなたの考えを深めてください。仲間と意見交換することによって、視野を広げることもできるでしょうし、自分の考えを見直すこともできるでしょう。そして、答えは必ずしもひとつではないことに気づくでしょう。

各ステップの問いやテーマは、私たちが考えたひとつの例に過ぎませんので、あまり縛られる必要はありません。話し合いの中でもっと良い「問い」をみつけたなら、ぜひクラスメイトととことん意見交換をし、考えを深めてください。そのような予期せぬ発見や発展に出会えることこそが協働学習の醍醐味です。

■ 振り返りと OUTPUT

大事なことは、各パッセージを読んだあとで必ず「振り返り」を行うことです。何を疑問に思い、何がわかったか、仲間のコメントから何を学び、自分の考えはどう変わったか、そうした学びのプロセスを振り返ってみましょう。振り返りによって、もやもやしていた自分の考えが明白になるかもしれません。そして、ひとつのパッセージを読み終わったときには、自分の考えが仲間に伝わるように英語で書いてみましょう。Output は学んだことを内化する（しっかり咀嚼して理解し自分の知識とする）ためにとても重要です。ユニットが進むにつれてだんだんに説得力のある英文が書けるようになるでしょう。しかし、このテキストは reading のテキストですので、たとえ writing のステップであっても paragraph の形式など細かい点に捕らわれる必要はありません。自分の考えを伝えることに焦点を当ててください。さらに、もし時間があれば、もうひとつの output 活動としてグループ・プレゼンテーションに挑戦してください。グループで話し合って、分担を決め、発表する内容をまとめ、練習してからクラスで発表するのです。できれば visual aid（絵や写真、パワーポイントなどの資料）も準備しましょう。聴衆（クラスメイト）もただ聞くのではなく、質問をし、お互いに評価し合いましょう。他のグループの考えを聞けばきっと新しい発見があるでしょう。みんなの前で発表するのは少し恥ずかしいかもしれませんが、工夫のある発表をして良い反応が得られれば自信がついて、もっと頑張ろうという気持ちになるだろうと思います。さらに、ユニットごとに組むメンバーを替えれば、違う仲間からまた新しいことが学べるでしょう。

■ おわりに

本テキストの12のパッセージを読み終わったとき、以前とは違う視点で世界を眺めているかもしれません。つまり、仲間とのやりとりを通して英語のパッセージを深く理解し、広い視野をもって読むことにより、日本語話者、英語話者といった区別ではなく、同じ人間として、一人ひとりが異なる論点をもつことを学んだのではないでしょうか。逆に、国籍・言語は違っても共通の感覚を持つことに気づいたかもしれません。あるいは、協働的な読みを通して、多角的で批判的な（critical）視点で世界を見直すことができるようになったかもしれません。さらに、自分の頭でじっくり考え、深く学ぶことの魅力に気づいたかもしれません。こうした英語学習を介して培われた思考を言語化する力や仲間と考えを共有する経験が、グローバル化がますます進むであろうこれからの社会で活躍なさる皆さんにとって大いに役立つことを心から願っています。

津田　ひろみ

注

[1]『協働で学ぶクリティカル・リーディング』（2015）舘岡洋子編著．ひつじ書房．

[2]『学校の挑戦：学びの共同体を創る』（2006）佐藤学．小学館．

本書のサポートページが、ひつじ書房のインターネットのサイトの中の

http://www.hituzi.co.jp/hituzibooks/ISBN978-4-89476-930-4.htm

にあります。

音源へのアクセスには、audiobook.jp の会員登録と以下のシリアルコード（数字）が必要になります。

69304

The support page for this book can be found at

http://www.hituzi.co.jp/hituzibooks/ISBN978-4-89476-930-4.htm

on the Hituzi Syobo website.

To access the sound source, you need to register at audiobook.jp and enter the following serial code (Digits).

69304

Wake up!

GETTING STARTED

Monkey Business Images/Shutterstock

Picture yourself in a typical class at university. What do you see? Maybe you imagine a scene like this: Students sit in rows all facing the front where the lecturer stands and talks. The lecturer might ask you questions or invite all of the students to ask questions. But most of the time, you just sit and listen. You may pay attention to what the lecturer is saying or demonstrating, but you may often find yourself thinking about something else. You might even drift off to sleep.

That is not the kind of class that this book is intended for.

To use this textbook effectively, you will need to sit facing your classmates, you will need to discuss together controversial issues and consider different ways of thinking about them. You will need to work on problems and think of better ways to solve them. Your teacher will facilitate your use of this book, will help guide and correct your comprehension and use of English, and will probably also contribute ideas and views to the discussion. But it is up to you to deepen and transform your own thinking. And it is up to you to use English as much as you can as you do this.

Above all, this will be a class where you think critically about the ideas that you encounter and collaborate with others. What does this mean exactly?

To begin with, critical thinking does not mean negative thinking. Rather it means thinking deeply and questioningly about everything you learn. As a critical thinker, you will need to identify the strengths and weaknesses of any new information or new ideas that you may encounter. More importantly, as a critical thinker, you need to be constantly mindful of the possibility that your own beliefs and knowledge may be limited and, if you are open to other ways of thinking, could be expanded and improved.

There is no single method of critical thinking, but a critical thinker needs to be aware of key principles that should underlie the communication of all ideas. Is the message clear, accurate, and precise? Is it consistent? Are the facts that are presented relevant and believable? Is the message conveyed with sufficient depth, breadth, and fairness? Not all these questions will apply to everything you will read or hear, but you need to bear them in mind at all times and notice if the answer to any of them is "no".

To be a critical thinker, you have to be independent and think for yourself. But you also have to realise that everyone is entitled to their own view. You need to try to understand the world as best you can and try to communicate your understanding to others, whilst always being sensitive to, and tolerant of others. No man is an island. All of us live in society, and in order to maintain and develop our society we have to work with others. Critical thinking on its own is not enough. You need to communicate your thinking to others, listen to and understand the thinking of others, and be flexible and gracious enough to appreciate better ideas. You also need to apply your thinking to the solution of problems. Sometimes, however good your ideas may be, they may not be suitable for the task at hand. Collaborating with others, you can examine a wider and more diverse range of ideas and apply them critically and fairly to the problems you solve together.

Picture yourself now in a critical collaborative reading class — in this class. Look at your fellow students. What will you learn from them? What will you learn with them? Aren't you curious? Let's begin.

Questions

Think about yourself now:

Do you think deeply about and question what you hear or read? When and why?
Do you accept what other people say without question? When and why?
How do you feel when you hear or read something you disagree with?

Discuss the meaning of the expression "no man is an island". Try to illustrate this with examples from your life or the life of someone you know.

How to use this textbook

As you have read in the previous section, this textbook is intended for collaborative and critical reading. To get the most out of this process, here are some tips and strategies:

Reading

The readings in this textbook are adapted from actual published texts and you may find them quite challenging.

- In order to maximise time for discussion in class, read the texts in your own time.
- Make sure you have time to read free from any interruptions.
- Check that you know the meanings of the words in the vocabulary exercise before starting the reading.
- Read through quickly to get the gist of the reading. Try to avoid using a dictionary at this stage. Guess the meaning of words or sentences you don't understand from the context of sentences that you do understand.
- Read through again and try to follow the author's argument and understand his or her purpose.
- Read the questions after each reading and make notes (in English) to help you prepare to discuss your answers in the class.
- If there is time in the class, refresh your memory of the reading before you discuss it by listening to the website that accompanies the textbook. You might find it useful to "shadow" the reading: while reading and listening, read aloud, whisper, or just imagine speaking aloud in unison with the speaker on the recording. The website's URL is https://audiobook.jp/exchange/hituzi/.

Warm-up

1. Pre-reading Questions

Think about some questions related to the theme of each reading and share your ideas with classmates.

2. Vocabulary Check

Guess the meaning of the vocabulary in the reading and confirm your answers with classmates and your teacher.

Understanding the Reading

Answer the questions related to the reading and compare your answers with classmates to deepen your understanding.

Getting the Main Idea

To make sure that you understand the passage, take notes about the main idea and the main points of the passage.

Compare your notes with your group members.

Personalizing

After discussing, write down what you think about the passage. Do you agree or disagree? Why?

Do you have any experience related to the main topic of the passage?

Sharing

Share your opinion and experience with your group members. Do you find any similarities and differences?

Critical Thinking & Reflection

Discuss with group members similarities and differences you have found through sharing ideas. In discussion, did you come across any new points of view?

Have you changed your idea after getting to know your classmates' opinions? Why or why not?

Expressing Your Ideas

Based on what you have learned from the passage and discussion, write your own ideas.

Explain your thinking to your group members.

Unit End Tasks (Option)

1. Opinion Writing

At the end of each unit, write your opinion about the theme of the unit.

2. Group Project

Give a short presentation with group members.

Alison Stewart

Nurture & Nature

UNIT ONE

Christos Georghiou/Shutterstock

Theme

Which has more influence on what we are, nurture or nature?

Reading 1 In Cross-Cultural Situations, Remember Those Emoticons (By Rowan Hooper) *The Japan Times* (2009/10/11)

Reading 2 Nurture as Important as Nature for Success (By Noah Smith) *The Japan Times* (2017/12/16)

Reading 3 It Begins at 10: How Gender Expectations Shape Early Adolescence Around the World (by Robert W. Blum, Kristin Mmari, and Caroline Moreau) *Journal of Adolescent Health* (2017/10)

Reading 1
In Cross-Cultural Situations, Remember Those Emoticons

Part 1 Warm-up

1. Pre-reading Questions

Think about the following questions and share your ideas with classmates.

1. Do you think facial expressions are universal? Why or why not?
2. Do you think humans and animals have similar facial expressions? Why or why not?
3. Have you ever noticed any difference in facial expressions among people with different cultural backgrounds? If so, what was the difference?

2. Vocabulary Check

Choose the correct definition from the two words inside the parentheses.

1. When my son was born, I **commenced** (a. started b. stopped) making notes of the various expressions which he exhibited.
2. This is a **quote** (a. question b. citation) from English naturalist Charles Darwin (1809-82).
3. Two things recently made me recall Darwin's work on facial expressions. The first was a remarkable meeting I had with one of his **descendants** (a. successors b. friends).
4. Keynes is 61 years old, and talking to him I was almost **spooked** (a. frightened b. disappointed).
5. Four generations on, I could clearly see the resemblance to his celebrated **ancestor** (a. forefather b. grandson).
6. East Asians have more trouble **distinguishing** (a. preventing b. telling) a face showing disgust from one that is displaying anger.
7. When examining a face, Easterners **fixate** (a. direct b. avoid) their attention on the eyes.
8. Does this **strike a chord with** (a. cause a similar reaction in b. cause a different reaction in) any Westerners living in Japan?
9. They then put them into categories: happy, sad, surprised, fearful, **disgusted** (a. pleased b. revolted), angry, or neutral.
10. The researchers say there are real **perceptual** (a. sensory b. emotional) differences between Western Caucasian and East Asian people.

Reading

In Cross-Cultural Situations, Remember Those Emoticons

1 "My first child was born on December 27th, 1839, and I at once **commenced** to make notes on the first dawn of the various expressions which he exhibited."

2 It will come as no surprise to many readers that this is a **quote** from the ever observant and curious English naturalist Charles Darwin (1809–82), originator of the Theory of Evolution by Natural Selection. He was convinced that all facial expressions were universal in all people, and even in animals, and that they must have a "gradual and natural origin." Darwin set out his argument in his book, "The Expression of the Emotions in Man and Animals," published in 1872. There he states his belief that, "The young and the old of widely different races, both with man and animals, express the same state of mind by the same movements."

3 Two things recently made me recall Darwin's work on facial expressions. The first was a remarkable meeting I had with one of his **descendants**, and the second was the publication of a study of differences in the interpretation of facial expressions between Westerners and East Asians.

4 I met Randal Keynes, Darwin's great-great grandson, in London, and we spoke about a film he has been involved with, titled "Creation," that is a story of Darwin's family life. Keynes is 61 years old, and talking to him I was almost **spooked**. Four generations on, I could clearly see the resemblance to his celebrated **ancestor**. Keynes is clean shaven and wears spectacles, but the eyes: his eyes are exactly the same as Charles Darwin's. In fact as I was talking with him — and I had to stop myself from referring to Darwin as "your great-great granddad" — he held my gaze as all the while I was thinking: "My god, he looks just like Darwin! It is Darwin!" What a shadow to grow up in — but what a considerate, thoughtful man Keynes was.

5 Then I came across a paper that challenges one of Darwin's arguments — that facial expressions are universal. As any Japanese who has lived in the West, or Westerner who has lived in Japan, will readily agree, there are obviously strong cultural differences at work in our societies. People from Japan and China generally have a tougher time than those from European countries in telling the difference between a face that looks fearful versus one that looks surprised. Similarly, East Asians have more trouble **distinguishing** a face showing disgust from one that is displaying anger.

6 Now scientists think they've figured it out: When examining a face, Easterners **fixate** their attention on the eyes, whereas Westerners scan evenly across the face.
"We show that Easterners and Westerners look at different face features to read facial expressions," said Rachael Jack of the University of Glasgow, in Scotland. "Westerners

look at the eyes and the mouth in equal measure, whereas Easterners favor the eyes and neglect the mouth. This means that Easterners have difficulty distinguishing facial expressions that look similar around the eye region."

7 The discovery shows that human communication of emotion is a lot more complex than we thought — and even than Darwin thought. As a result, facial expressions that had been considered universally recognizable cannot be used to reliably convey emotion in cross-cultural situations. Does this **strike a chord with** any Westerners living in Japan? Or Japanese when interacting with Westerners?

8 Certainly, I can understand it. There are many occasions when expressions and emotions may be misunderstood, and this research might provide part of an explanation as to why that happens so frequently.

9 Jack and colleagues investigated cultural differences in the recognition of facial expressions by recording the eye movements of 13 Western Caucasian and 13 East Asian people while they observed pictures of expressive faces. They then put them into categories: happy, sad, surprised, fearful, **disgusted**, angry, or neutral. The faces were standardized according to something called the Facial Action Coding System (FACS). This sets each expression as displaying a specific combination of facial muscles typically associated with each feeling of emotion. The researchers then compared how accurately participants read those facial expressions using their particular eye-movement strategies.

10 It turned out that Easterners focused much greater attention on the eyes, and made significantly more errors than Westerners did. In other words, while Westerners use the whole face to convey emotion, Easterners use the eyes more and the mouth less. And interestingly, this cultural difference extends to cyberspace. Emoticons — text marks used to convey facial expressions of the writer's mood — are different in Japan and the West. In the West, the commonest emoticons for "happy" and "sad" use the mouth to convey the emotion, so we have :) and :(In Japan, however, the eyes are used to convey the emotions, so ^.^ is commonly used for happy and ;-; for sad. "Emoticons are used to convey different emotions in cyberspace as they are the iconic representation of facial expressions," Jack said. "Interestingly, there are clear cultural differences in the formations of these icons."

11 In summary, the researchers say, there are real **perceptual** differences between Western Caucasian and East Asian people. However, I doubt whether that applies to Caucasians who have grown up in Japan, or Japanese who have grown up in America, for example. It's all about the culture you grow up in — your so-called nurture rather than nature.

12 But, without overgeneralizing, it does help us understand how attempts to communicate emotions sometimes get lost in translation.

Part 2 Understanding the Reading

Answer the following questions. Then compare your answers with classmates.

1. What do you think Darwin found by observing his child's various expressions?

2. Darwin argued, "The young and the old of widely different races, both with man and animals, express the same state of mind by the same movements." (paragraph 2) Do you think this is true?

3. Why was the author of this article so surprised when he saw Darwin's great-great grandson?

4. Why is it difficult for East Asians to tell the difference between a fearful expression and a surprised expression?

5. What is the main difference between the facial expressions of Westerners and those of Easterners?

6. What is the difference between the emoticons in the West and those in Japan?

7. Do you think the facial expressions of Japanese who have grown up in America are similar to those of Japanese or those of Americans?

8. What does the author mean by stating "it does help us understand how attempts to communicate emotions sometimes get lost in translation"? (paragraph 12)

UNIT ONE

Part 3  Getting the Main Idea

1. To make sure that you understand the passage, take notes about the main idea and the main points.

2. Compare your notes with your group members.

Part 4 Personalizing

1. This article reports a research finding that "while Westerners use the whole face to convey emotion, Easterners use the eyes more and the mouth less." Do you think this applies to yourself? Write down your idea.

____

____

____

____

2. Which do you think has more impact on one's facial expressions, nature or nurture? Why do you think so?

____

____

____

____

____

Part 5 Sharing

Share your opinion with your group members about the author's viewpoint. Did you find any interesting ideas from your classmates? What are they? What do you think?

Part 6 Critical Thinking & Reflection

It's reflection time!

1. Discuss with group members similarities and differences you have found through sharing ideas. In discussion, did you come across any new points of view?

2. Have you changed your idea after getting to know your classmates' opinions? Why or why not?

Part 7 Expressing Your Ideas

Write down your own opinion about the theme of this article, "Facial expressions are influenced by the culture we live in." Use your notes to explain your thinking to your group members.

____

____

____

____

____

____

Reading 2
Nurture as Important as Nature for Success

Part 1 Warm-up

1. Pre-reading Questions

Think about the following questions and share your ideas with classmates.

1. Do you think natural ability is a more decisive factor for success than effort? Explain.
2. Do you think men are better at math than women by nature? Explain.
3. Do you think education could raise one's IQ? Explain.

2. Vocabulary Check

1. Fill the blanks with the appropriate words listed below.

slacking	lamented	disparity	assault	primacy

1) The (   ) between rich and poor keeps widening.

2) The teacher (   ) his students' lack of motivation.

3) Many people understand the (   ) of education in a person's life.

4) His new theory came under (   ) from other researchers.

5) He was scolded for (   ) while others were trying hard.

2. Match the words with their definitions

1) fuel	a. very strong
2) subscribe to	b. the way a person typically thinks about things
3) mindset	c. difficult
4) arbitrary	d. inborn
5) robust	e. agree to
6) fraught	f. boost
7) innate	g. random

Reading

Nurture as Important as Nature for Success

1 The question of nature versus nurture is an important one, but also an incredibly delicate one.

2 How much of the **disparities** we see in society are **fueled** by a lack of good education, social influences and role models, and how much are due to natural ability? Given that people in advanced countries spend multiple decades of their life in school, this is an important question.

3 But it's also a very **fraught** one — discussions about the issue are frequently hijacked by people pushing racist or sexist theories, and polite society's reaction, understandably, is often to make such discussions taboo.

4 As a result, it's hard to know what people really think about the nature-versus-nurture question. My impression is that most Americans **subscribe to** a casual, reflexive faith in the **primacy** of inborn ability. Several years ago, my doctoral adviser Miles Kimball and I wrote a widely read article **lamenting** American students' lack of effort in mathematics. We believe that many Americans don't try hard because they believe that all math skill is **innate** — a "fixed **mindset**," as described by Stanford University psychologist Carol Dweck.

5 Some recent research appears to support the first part of our hypothesis. Bentley University economist Jeff Livingston found that paying American students cash incentives causes them to do better on the PISA, an international standardized test of math skills. But similar incentives had no effect on Chinese students, implying that Americans are **slacking** while Chinese students are trying hard.

6 So effort matters. But what about education itself ? There is a common belief that life outcomes are heavily determined by IQ. And many websites will confidently tell you that "your IQ score is relatively stable, no matter what education you acquire." But this is false. Some startling new research shows that education actually raises IQ substantially.

7 Psychologists Stuart Ritchie and Elliot Tucker-Drob have a new meta-analysis of papers that study the effect of education on IQ. Because smarter people can be motivated to stay in school longer, Ritchie and Tucker-Drob consider only studies that use natural experiments — things like policy changes, or **arbitrary** cutoffs, that determine how much classroom time people get. Altogether, the studies they survey represent 600,000 people — a huge sample. They wrote:
"We found consistent evidence for beneficial effects of education on cognitive abilities, of approximately 1 to 5 IQ points for an additional year of education.... (T)he effects

persisted across the life span, and were present on all broad categories of cognitive ability studied. Education appears to be the most consistent, **robust**, and durable method yet to be identified for raising intelligence."

8 Since the standard deviation of IQ is 15 points (most scores are between 85 and 115), a one- to five-point improvement per year of education is an absolutely enormous effect. Ritchie and Tucker-Drob's result doesn't mean that nature doesn't matter at all — it clearly does — but it indicates that nurture, in the form of education, is extremely powerful.

9 How about the notion that smarts determine life success? That idea too has come under **assault** from recent research. A recent paper by economists Alex Bell, Raj Chetty, Xavier Jaravel, Neviana Petkova and John Van Reenen — a star-studded list of names — finds that at least for certain kinds of achievement, factors other than natural ability matter quite a lot.

10 Bell et al. study invention — specifically, how many patents someone has to their name. Invention is different from innovation and patents aren't a good measure of how economically useful a discovery is. But patenting does measure a specific kind of intellectually demanding, rigorous and often highly compensated form of work — if you get a job doing something that involves being awarded a patent, chances are that your economic situation is pretty solid.

11 Since mental ability matters for invention, Bell et al. control for performance on childhood math tests. But huge gaps remain — between rich and poor, and between white men and other demographic groups. Poor people, women and minorities all produce many fewer patents than wealthy white men with equivalent math test scores.

12 What explains the difference? Bell et al. think that human influence matters a lot. They find that even controlling for math ability, people whose parents are inventors tend to become inventors themselves. Neighborhoods also matter; people who grow up around a lot of inventors tend to become inventors when they grow up.
Bell et al. don't have the data to study role models — who kids see on TV or on the internet doing science and engineering. Nor can they observe the mentors that people encounter in their adult life. But the effects of parents and neighborhoods imply that role models and adult mentors might also be key reasons why women and minorities are underrepresented among the ranks of inventors.

13 So many different kinds of nurture matter in determining success. Effort matters. Education matters. And social environment matters. Americans discount these factors too much. The country would be a better, richer, more equal place with less emphasis on natural talent and more on humans' potential to improve each other and themselves.

Part 2 Understanding the Reading

Answer the following questions. Then compare your answers with classmates.

1. What does the author mean by "hijacked by people pushing racist or sexist theories"? (paragraph 3)

2. What does the author mean by "polite society's reaction"? (paragraph 3)

3. Why does the author think American students don't try hard in mathematics?

4. How did Jeff Livingstone discover that American students actually tend to make less effort than Chinese students?

5. What is a common belief of Americans about the relation between success in life and IQ?

6. What did Ritchie and Tucker's study find about the effects of education on intelligence?

7. What did Alex Bell and his fellow economists try to establish by studying invention?

8. According to Bell et al., why did poor people, women and minorities produce fewer patents than wealthy white men?

Part 3  Getting the Main Idea

1. To make sure that you understand the passage, take notes about the main idea and the main points.

2. Compare your notes with your group members.

Part 4 Personalizing

1. What are you good at? (e.g., sports, music, cooking, etc.) What do you think is the reason you are good at it : natural ability, effort, education, or social environment?

2. How do you think your life has been influenced by the following factors : natural ability, effort, education, and social environment?

Part 5 Sharing

Share your opinion with your group members about the author's viewpoint. Did you find any interesting ideas from your classmates? What are they? What do you think?

Part 6 Critical Thinking & Reflection

It's reflection time!

1. Discuss with group members similarities and differences you have found through sharing ideas. In discussion, did you come across any new points of view?

2. Have you changed your idea after getting to know your classmates' opinions? Why or why not?

Part 7 Expressing Your Ideas

Write down your own opinion about the theme of this reading, "Nurture is as important as nature in explaining success in life." Use your notes to explain your thinking to your group members.

Reading 3

It Begins at 10: How Gender Expectations Shape Early Adolescence Around the World

Part 1 Warm-up

1. Pre-reading Questions

Think about the following questions and share your ideas with classmates.

1. Do you think teenage girls are weaker than boys and they need more protection? Explain.
2. Do you have any experience of having your behavior restricted because you are a boy or a girl? Explain.
3. Do you have a friend of the opposite gender? Do you think it is possible for a boy and a girl to have a real friendship? Explain.

2. Vocabulary Check

Fill the blanks with the appropriate words listed below.

legitimate	vulnerable	tolerant	sanctions	adolescence
consequences	embodiment	norms	predators	expectancy

1) (   ) is the period during which a young person develops from a child into an adult.
2) Health and well-being in teens influences health trajectories with lifelong (   ).
3) The dominant myth is that girls are (   ) and that boys are strong and independent.
4) Around the world teenaged boys are viewed as (   ) and girls as potential targets and victims.
5) Teenage girls tend to be seen as the (   ) of sex and sexuality.
6) Girls are repeatedly told to stay away from boys and there are (   ) if they do not, such as punishment, social isolation, and sexual rumor.
7) Boys and girls played together as children and were friends, but now with puberty, these friendships are no longer (   ).
8) The data suggest that boys are even less (   ) of peers whose interests or appearances are more typical of the opposite sex than their own.
9) Gender (   ) and beliefs have significant implications for both girls and boys.
10) In fact, men's life (   ) is shorter than that of women.

Reading

It Begins at 10: How Gender Expectations Shape Early Adolescence Around the World

1 The period of **adolescence** (ages 10-19 years) is one of the most critical periods of human development as the health and well-being at this age influences health trajectories with lifelong consequences. While considered among the healthiest period of the lifespan, the period of early adolescence (ages10-14 years) is also a transitional period in which many health behaviors are acquired. However, this has been greatly overlooked. To address this gap, in the fall of 2011, a group of six research teams met in Dakar, Senegal, to begin conceptualizing a study focused on early adolescents. A year earlier, the World Health Organization convened an expert committee to specifically identify the priorities for adolescent health; and the paucity of research on early adolescence was identified as a primary gap. In Dakar, gender inequalities and their **consequences** for sexual and reproductive health and health more broadly emerged as top priorities. Over the nearly 4 years that followed, the initial group of country collaborators grew to 15 from across five continents (Ecuador, Bolivia, Belgium, Scotland, United States, South Africa, Malawi, Kenya, DR Congo, Burkina Faso, Nigeria, Egypt, Vietnam, China, and India). At that time, there was little understanding of or prior research on how to conceptualize or measure key constructs related to gender **norms**, relationships, sexuality, and empowerment in early adolescence. To better understand the gendered transitions from childhood to adolescence we decided to start the Global Early Adolescent Study by asking young people and their parents about their experiences of growing up as a boy or girl in their communities. Grounded in the voices of young people and parents, the present special supplement captures some of the cross-cutting themes about these transitions across locations and continents. What did we hear?

2

1. The hegemonic myth: There is a global set of forces from schools, parents, media, and peers themselves that reinforce the hegemonic myths that girls are **vulnerable** and that boys are strong and independent. Even in sites where parents acknowledged the vulnerability of their sons, they focus on protecting their daughters.
2. Pubertal girls are the **embodiment** of sex and sexuality: Around the world pubertal boys are viewed as **predators** and girls as potential targets and victims. Messages such as — do not sit like that, do not wear that, do not talk to him, boys will ruin your future — support the gender division of power and affect while promote sex segregation to preserve girl's sexuality. In some places, girls come to internalize these norms to even a greater extent than boys.

3. Cover up and do not go out: As a consequence of adult perceptions of female sexual vulnerability, in nearly every site, girls' mobility is far more restricted than for boys. As one girl in Assuit, Egypt noted: "A girl cannot go out as she wishes because she is a girl and if a girl came home late her parents would shout at her, but it is okay for a guy."
4. Boys are trouble: Because of adult concerns about their sexual vulnerability, girls are repeatedly told to stay away from boys and there are **sanctions** if they do not — punishment, social isolation, sexual rumor, and innuendo. Both boys and girls lament this situation. They played together as children and were friends, but now with puberty, those friendships are no longer **legitimate**.
5. Both boys and girls are aware of gender nonconforming peers: Young people (as well as a number of parents) spoke of peers whose interests, appearance, dress, and/or appearance was more typical of the opposite sex than their own. For such young people, there were significant sanctions and pressures to conform to what is seen as gender-appropriate behaviors; and our quantitative data suggest that boys are even less **tolerant** of such peers than girls.

3 Gender norms and beliefs have significant implications for both girls and boys. The consequences for girls in many parts of the world include child marriage, early school leaving, pregnancy, HIV and sexually transmitted infection risk, violence exposure, and depression. But despite popular perceptions boys are not unscathed. As a result of these hegemonic norms, they engage in and are the victims of physical violence to a much greater extent than girls; they die more frequently from unintentional injuries, are more prone to substance abuse and suicide; and as adults their life **expectancy** is shorter than that of women. Such differences are socially not biologically determined. As young people grow up to become men and women, they engage with and construct their own gender-based understandings of what it means to be a boy or a girl. This process is amenable to change by fostering gender equitable approaches that have the potential to improve the well-being of adolescent boys and adolescent girls in the short and long terms. That is the challenge ahead of us but first let us listen carefully to what young people and their parents and guardians are telling us.

Part 2 Understanding the Reading

Answer the following questions. Then compare your answers with classmates.

1. Why is adolescence viewed as one of the most critical periods of human development?

2. In the 5th line of the 1st paragraph, the author writes, "However, this has been greatly overlooked." (paragraph 1) What has been overlooked?

3. What approach did the collaborative study group take to better understand the gendered transitions from childhood to adolescence?

4. Why is girls' mobility far more restricted than for boys around the world?

5. What consequences do gender norms and beliefs bring about in many parts of the world?

6. Why are boys more likely to be exposed to violence, die from unintentional injuries and are more prone to abuse and suicide than girls?

7. What does the author mean by saying "Such differences are socially not biologically determined"? (paragraph 3)

8. What kind of solution does the author suggest for improving the well-being of adolescent boys and girls?

Part 3 Getting the Main Idea

1. To make sure that you understand the passage, take notes about the main idea and the main points.

2. Compare your notes with your group members.

Part 4 Personalizing

1. Do you think you have been affected by any kinds of gender norms and beliefs? What kind of norms and beliefs are they? Write down your idea and give some examples that support your idea.

2. What would you feel if there is a classmate whose appearance or interest is more typical of the opposite sex than his/her own? Explain.

Part 5 Sharing

Share your opinion with your group members about the author's viewpoint. Did you find any interesting ideas from your classmates? What are they? What do you think?

Part 6 Critical Thinking & Reflection

It's reflection time!

1. Discuss with group members similarities and differences you have found through sharing ideas. In discussion, did you come across any new points of view?

2. Have you changed your idea after getting to know your classmates' opinions? Why or why not?

Part 7 Expressing Your Ideas

Write down your own opinion about the theme of this reading, "Gender norms and beliefs have significant consequences for both girls and boys." Use your notes to explain your thinking to your group members.

____

____

____

____

____

____

UNIT END TASKS

Choose one of the following tasks.

1. OPINION WRITING

Write your opinion on the theme of this unit: Which has more influence on what we are, nurture or nature? Illustrate your ideas with examples from the readings in this textbook or from your own research.

2. GROUP PROJECT

Search for information on how non-verbal communication (e.g., eye contact gestures, interpersonal distance, etc.) is different from culture to culture. Compile the collected information and give a short presentation to the class.

Group & Individual

UNIT TWO

VoodooDot/Shutterstock

Theme

How can you contribute to making a better society?

Reading 1 The Secret to Smart Groups: It's Women (by Derek Thompson) *The Atlantic* (2015/01/18)

Reading 2 Japanese Firms Need More Diverse Workforce, Says Harvard Academic (by Magdalena Osumi) *The Japan Times* (2015/09/15)

Reading 3 The Power of Introverts: A Manifesto for Quiet Brilliance (by Gareth Cook) *Scientific American* (2012/01/24)

Reading 1

The Secret to Smart Groups: It's Women

Part 1 Warm-up

1. Pre-reading Questions

Think about the following questions and share your ideas with classmates.

1. What factors do you think are important for a successful group?
2. What do you think are some advantages or disadvantages of working together in a group?
3. How do you tend to behave in a group? Do you often assert yourself? Do you listen to others attentively?

2. Vocabulary Check

Guess the meaning of the bold-faced words from the context and choose the best one.

1) … we find **converging** evidence of a general collective intelligence factor that explains a group's performance on a wide variety of tasks.

a. different　　b. leading to the same conclusion　　c. supporting

2) This "c factor" is not strongly **correlated** with the average or maximum individual intelligence of group members.…

a. well supported　　b. calculated correctly　　c. closely related

3) First, neither the average intelligence of the group nor the smartest person in the group **had much to do with** the group's "c" factor.

a. were necessary for　　b. was closely related with　　c. were responsible for

4) … the predictable troupe of buzzwords you would expect to correlate with successful groups — "**cohesion**," "motivation," and "satisfaction" — didn't have much to do with effective teams, either.

a. unity　　b. intelligence　　c. praise

5) That is, the best groups were also the best at reading the **non-verbal** cues of their teammates.

a. emotional　　b. not using words　　c. rude

6) ...it **turns out** that women are naturally more fluent in the language of tone and faces than the other half of their species.

a. is discovered b. is apparent c. is not accepted

7) Isn't it possible that there are specific personality traits — like openness or **empathy** — that might make some men just as good as women at reading the minds of their teammates?

a. being cheerful b. being brave
c. having the ability to understand others' feelings

8) Second, the relationship between smart teammates and smart groups is **complicated** by the fact that groups are sometimes assigned problems that only require one person to solve.

a. made difficult b. disturbed c. supported

9) First, there is a growing sense that the Internet can destroy **interpersonal** skills, kill our emotional intelligence, and turn us into warm-blooded versions of the very robots that we fear will one day take our jobs.

a. between people b. focused on an individual c. creative

10) Third, men might have innate disadvantages in collaborative work settings, like the emotional illiteracy **alluded** to in these studies.

a. suggested b. discovered c. falsified

Reading

The Secret to Smart Groups: It's Women

1 The concept of "general intelligence"—the idea that people who are good at one mental task tend to be good at many others—was considered radical in 1904, when Charles Spearman proposed the theory of a "g factor." Today, however, it is among the most replicated findings in psychology. But whereas in 1904 the U.S. economy was a network of farms, mills, and artisans, today's economy is an office-based affair, where the most important *g* for many companies doesn't stand for *g*eneral intelligence, but, rather, *g*roups.

2 So, what makes groups smart? Is there any such thing as a "smart" group, or are groups just, well, clumps of smart people?

3 As a team of scientists from MIT, Carnegie Mellon, and Union College write in the *New York Times*, research suggests that just as some individuals are smarter than others, some groups are smarter than others, across a range of tests and tasks. In other words, there is a "c factor" for *c*ollective intelligence. Teams that are successful at solving visual puzzles also tend to be good at brainstorming *and* beating computers in video games.

4 In two studies with 699 people, working in groups of two to five, we find **converging** evidence of a general collective intelligence factor that explains a group's performance on a wide variety of tasks. This "c factor" is not strongly **correlated with** the average or maximum individual intelligence of group members but is correlated with the average social sensitivity of group members, the equality in distribution of conversational turn-taking, and the proportion of females in the group.

5 That bolded sentence is hiding a lot of heavy conclusions in plain sight. First, neither the average intelligence of the group nor the smartest person in the group **had much to do with** the group's "c" factor. Just as great artists don't necessarily form great bands when they pool their talents, smart people don't automatically make smart groups.

6 Furthermore, the predictable troupe of buzzwords you would expect to correlate with successful groups—"**cohesion**," "motivation," and "satisfaction"—didn't have much to do with effective teams, either. Instead, the single most important element of smart groups, according to the researchers, was their "average social sensitivity." That is, the best groups were also the best at reading the non-verbal cues of their teammates. And, since women score higher on this metric of emotional intelligence, teams with more women tended to be better teams.

7 What the heck is *average social sensitivity*? It is, essentially, mind-reading. When a member of your team—Michelle, we'll call her—says "I guess Danny really does have the answer for everything," and you detect a hint of aggrieved irony in Michelle's

statement, while further noting the simultaneous drop in Michelle's chin as she makes the comment, coinciding with a deflated air of preemptive surrender in Michelle's tone, and you begin to think, *hmmm, maybe what Michelle is actually saying is that Danny is a know-it-all jerk?*, you are detecting what scientists would call "**non-verbal** clues." In plain-speak, you are reading between the lines. Indeed, like reading, social sensitivity is a kind of literacy, and it **turns out** that women are naturally more fluent in the language of tone and faces than the other half of their species.

8 Women are better at reading the mind through the face even online, when they can't see their teammates' faces. In a follow-up study, the scientists gave participants a "Reading the Mind in the Eyes," or RME, test, where they were asked to identify complex emotions (e.g., shame or curiosity, rather than sadness or joy) in pictures of other people's eyes. Then they divided participants into teams and had them perform a number of tests, like brainstorming and group Sudoku. Again, teams with more women, who scored higher on the RME test, performed the best across the tasks. From the paper:

9 The [RME] scores of group members were a strong predictor of how well the groups could perform a wide range of tasks together, even when participants were only collaborating online via text chat and could not see each other's eyes or facial expressions at all.

10 Reading these studies, I could think of two obvious objections.

- First: Isn't it possible that there are specific personality traits—like openness or **empathy**—that might make some men just as good as women at reading the minds of their teammates?
- Second: Is it really true that smarter teammates have so little to do with smart groups?

11 The researchers answer the first question explicitly, with a *no*. "We found no significant correlation between a general factor of personality and collective intelligence or RME," they write. Mind-reading isn't a personality trait. It's a skill.

12 Second, the relationship between smart teammates and smart groups is **complicated** by the fact that groups are sometimes assigned problems that only require one person to solve. If you ask a team of highly emotionally sensitive people to solve a differential calculus problem, and none of them knows calculus, it's unlikely that they will come to grasp Taylor polynomials*1 by looking deeply into each others' eyes and really, truly *listening*. When the problem can be solved by one really smart cookie (e.g., who remembers calculus), it's nice to have a really smart cookie. If, however, the solution requires deep collaboration, EQ*2 trumps IQ*3.

13 I found these studies eye-opening for two further reasons. First, there is a growing sense that the Internet can destroy **interpersonal** skills, kill our emotional intelligence, and turn us into warm-blooded versions of the very robots that we fear will one day take our jobs. But these studies suggest that the rules of empathy hold both on- and offline. Emotionally sensitive people are gifted at reading between the lines, whether the literal lines are brow wrinkles or text messages.

14 Second, if you take these findings seriously, they represent a third fork of evidence suggesting that the male-female gender wage gap will not only close but also invert. It would surprise me if, in a generation, women aren't earning more than men across many mainstream industries.

15 First, women earn the majority of bachelor's degrees, Master's degrees, and Ph.D's. The historical relationship between higher education and earnings is simple: Those who learn more earn more. This advantage will continue to enrich women in the labor force. Second, if you look at the direction of job growth, brawny, muscly jobs like construction and manufacturing are in structural decline, while the fastest growing jobs, both at the low-pay end and in the white-collar world, require softer skills where men have no physical advantage. Third, men might have innate disadvantages in collaborative work settings, like the emotional illiteracy **alluded** to in these studies.

*Notes

1 Taylor polynomial: a technical term for mathematics, an approximation of a function using terms from the functions Taylor series.

2 EQ stands for "emotional quotient."

3 IQ stands for "intelligent quotient."

Part 2 Understanding the Reading

Answer the following questions. Then compare your answers with classmates.

1. What is "general intelligence"?

2. What is "collective intelligence"?

3. What is "average social sensitivity"?

4. According to the team of scientists mentioned in the reading, what factors contribute to a successful group? Among them, what do they think is the most important factor for success?

5. How does the writer describe characteristics usually associated with women? How do those characteristics contribute to a successful group?

6. What is the purpose of the RME test?

7. The writer says, "Emotionally sensitive people are gifted at reading between the lines, whether the literal lines are brow wrinkles or text messages." (paragraph 13) What does he mean by "brow wrinkles"?

8. What change does the writer think will occur in a future society? Why does he think this?

Part 3 Getting the Main Idea

1. To make sure that you understand the passage, take notes about the main idea and the main points.

2. Compare your notes with your group members.

Part 4 Personalizing

1. Do you agree with the idea that more women make a smarter group? Why or why not?

2. What experience have you had where women or men influenced the way the group operated?

Part 5 Sharing

Share your opinion with your group members about the author's viewpoint. Did you find any interesting ideas from classmates? What are they? What do you think?

Part 6 Critical Thinking & Reflection

It's reflection time!

1. Discuss with group members similarities and differences you have found through sharing ideas. In discussion, did you come across any new points of view?

2. Have you changed your idea after getting to know your classmates' opinions? Why or why not?

Part 7 Expressing Your Ideas

Write down your own opinion about the claim that more women make a smarter group. Use your notes to explain your thinking to your group members.

____

____

____

____

____

____

Reading 2

Japanese Firms Need More Diverse Workforce, Says Harvard Academic

Part 1 Warm-up

1. Pre-reading Questions

Think about the following questions and share your ideas with classmates.

1. Do you feel comfortable or uncomfortable when speaking up in a group? What kinds of group make you feel this way?
2. What kinds of people do you think will be included in a diversified workforce?
3. Who are some examples of good leaders? Why do you think they are good leaders?

2. Vocabulary Check

Guess the meaning of the bold-faced words from the context and choose the best one.

1) The recent passage of a **bill** requiring companies to set numerical goals in hiring and promoting women should improve the working environment for them.

   a. official notice　　b. suggestion for a new law　　c. command

2) Japan still **has far to go** in creating the kind of diversified workplace needed for innovation.

   a. has a lot of work to do　　b. has a wrong way　　c. has a lot of interest

3) … they [women] are less likely to be viewed as potential **visionaries** because of their different approach to problem-solving.

   a. adventurers　　b. forward-looking people　　c. leaders

4) **Prejudice** could cloud judgment when companies hire or promote female workers.

   a. a wrong idea　　b. a reasonable belief　　c. an unfair opinion

5) Hill describes this as collaborative problem-solving among people of different backgrounds and **expertise**.

   a. exceptional talent　　b. high intelligence　　c. expert knowledge and skill

6) To sustain success you need more leaders who know how to develop talent that would know how to do what's necessary, leaders who know how to **embrace** diversity more.

   a. reject　　b. creates　　c. accept

7) Japan needs leaders who can **get the most out of** diverse thinking so they can indeed innovate.

a. make full use of　　b. admire　　c. fully understand

8) Whether or not that diversity is celebrated and **amplified** depends on (who) at the top looks at those ideas.

a. appreciated　　b. promoted　　c. spoiled

9) … such attempts may be difficult at established companies because workers are afraid of **losing face**.

a. being yelled at　　b. making a mistake　　c. being humiliated

10) … if you can't have that debate, you don't get a **robust** marketplace of ideas.

a. innovative　　b. strong　　c. abundant

Reading

Japanese Firms Need More Diverse Workforce, Says Harvard Academic

1 The recent passage of a **bill** requiring companies to set numerical goals in hiring and promoting women should improve the working environment for them, a Harvard Business School professor has said.

But Linda Hill cautions that Japan still **has far to go** in creating the kind of diversified workplace needed for innovation.

"Transparency will put companies under pressure ... and it will allow women to make choices," said Linda Hill, a guest panelist at the World Assembly for Women in Tokyo last month, speaking to The Japan Times.

2 For Japanese companies to be innovative, they need to create a workplace where women can demonstrate their potential, said Hill, co-author of "Collective Genius," which examines the work of leading innovators.

She said problems might emerge once more women join companies, as they are less likely to be viewed as potential **visionaries** because of their different approach to problem-solving.

"My worry is, do we know how to evaluate those women," she said.

3 **Prejudice** could cloud judgment when companies hire or promote female workers, at times depriving them of the opportunity to climb the corporate ladder, said Hill, an expert on corporate leadership.

In the past, American companies would reject female applicants who did not play team sports, Hill said, as they presumed the women would not be good leaders.

4 Companies need to offer opportunities for female workers to learn how to lead and demonstrate their potential if firms want to diversify their workplace, she said.

And the role of corporate leaders is to create an environment that triggers innovation: Hill describes this as collaborative problem-solving among people of different backgrounds and **expertise**.

"To sustain success you need more leaders who know how to develop talent that would know how to do what's necessary, leaders who know how to **embrace** diversity more," she said. "Japan needs leaders who can **get the most out of** diverse thinking so they can indeed innovate."

5 Hill has observed Japanese companies trying to change their managerial strategies and to become more innovative. These include Mitsubishi Corp., where Japanese workers including executives are required to communicate with colleagues from other countries in English.

"Whether or not that diversity is celebrated and **amplified** depends on (who) at the top looks at those ideas," Hill said.

6 The tight chain of command common in Japanese corporate culture may also make it difficult for innovative ideas to reach senior management decision-makers.

"In such cultures, you're much more likely to have people think things need to be fairly top-down: I'm the one who leads and you're the one who follows," she said. In those cases, employees tend to wait for instructions rather than making proposals on their own.

7 Hill has spent more than a decade studying some of the world's most creative companies, including Google Inc.

She believes Japanese employers need to create an environment where workers feel "enough psychological safety" to have the confidence to submit ideas to their supervisors.

"We know that most … (attempts at innovation) don't actually work. They're false starts," Hill said, noting that such attempts may be difficult at established companies because workers are afraid of **losing face**.

She said Japan is not the only country where business leaders struggle to maintain a balance between the chain of command and workers who seek to convey innovative ideas to decision makers.

8 One theory of management, that of visionary leadership, created in the U.S. in the 1990s and adopted by many firms as a managerial strategy, states that all leaders need a vision of a better future. The leader pursues a top-down approach to achieve the corporate goal.

"But if you want to build an organization that can innovate, you have to figure out how to balance that with a more bottom-up approach, since most innovation comes from collaborative work."

9 She stressed that differences should be amplified, not minimized.

"The idea that you have conflict, that you need to be able to debate those ideas, is one of the parts of the puzzle that would be more difficult because of the culture (in Japan) and particularly across levels," Hill said. "And if you can't have that debate, you don't get a **robust** marketplace of ideas."

Part 2 Understanding the Reading

Answer the following questions. Then compare your answers with classmates.

1. What does Linda Hill mean by saying "Transparency will put companies under pressure" (paragraph 1)?

2. What is one concern Hill has for women's increased participation in the workforce?

3. According to Hill, what was a common prejudice against female workers in the U.S?

4. What type of corporate leaders does Hill think will encourage innovation?

5. According to Hill, what is a Japanese cultural factor that stifles innovation?

6. What does Hill mean by "enough psychological safety (paragraph 7)?

7. Why does Hill stress that "differences should be amplified, not minimized (paragraph 9)" in collaborative work?

8. What does Linda Hill think will be necessary for Japanese companies to be innovative?

Part 3 Getting the Main Idea

1. To make sure that you understand the passage, take notes about the main idea and the main points.

2. Compare your notes with your group members.

Part 4 Personalizing

1. Do you agree with the idea that the workforce should be diversified to encourage innovation? Why or why not?

____

____

____

____

2. Have you ever felt or not felt "psychological safety" in voicing your opinions in a group? Describe your experiences.

____

____

____

____

____

Part 5 Sharing

Share your opinion with your group members about the author's viewpoint. Did you find any interesting ideas from your classmates? What are they? What do you think?

Part 6 Critical Thinking & Reflection

It's reflection time!

1. Discuss with group members similarities and differences you have found through sharing ideas. In discussion, did you come across any new points of view?

2. Have you changed your idea after getting to know your classmates' opinions? Why or why not?

Part 7 Expressing Your Ideas

Write down your own opinion about the theme of this reading, "the importance of diversification for an innovative workforce and the role of managers in promoting diversity." Use your notes to explain your thinking to your group members.

____

____

____

____

____

____

Reading 3

The Power of Introverts: A Manifesto for Quiet Brilliance

Part 1 Warm-up

1. Pre-reading Questions

Think about the following questions and share your ideas with classmates.

1. What comes to your mind when you hear the word "solitude"? Do you have a positive or negative feeling about the word?
2. Do you like working alone in a quiet place or working together with friends in a group to solve problems?
3. What do you think are some advantages or disadvantages of working alone?

2. Vocabulary Check

Guess the meaning of the bold-faced words from the context and choose the best one.

1) We live in a nation that values its **extroverts** — the outgoing, the lovers of crowds — but not the quiet types who change the world.

   a. a person who turns outward　　b. a person who turns inward
   c. a responsible person

2) **Introverts** prefer quiet, minimally stimulating environments, while extroverts need higher levels of stimulation to feel their best.

   a. people who are very sociable　　b. people who prefer to be alone
   c. creative people

3) Shyness is **inherently** uncomfortable; introversion is not.

   a. essentially　　b. partly　　c. very

4) In my book, I travel the country — from a Tony Robbins seminar to Harvard Business School to Rick Warren's powerful Saddleback Church — **shining a light on** the bias against introversion.

   a. understanding　　b. exposing　　c. objecting to

5) Introverts are constantly going to parties and such when they'd really prefer to be home reading, studying, inventing, **meditating**, designing, thinking, cooking…or any number of other quiet and worthwhile activities.

   a. relaxing　　b. playing　　c. thinking deeply

6) It's never a good idea to organize society in a way that **depletes** the energy of half the population.

a. takes advantage of　　b. reduces a great amount of　　c. puts a heavy burden on

7) …, and in my book I examine lots of research on the **pitfalls** of groupwork.

a. hidden dangers　　b. unexpected advantages　　c. misuses

8) We're such social animals that we **instinctively** mimic others' opinions, often without realizing we're doing it.

a. based on intuition　　b. unexpectedly　　c. before we know it

9) People sometimes seem surprised when I say this, because I'm a pretty friendly person. This is one of the greatest **misconceptions** about introversion.

a. mistreatments　　b. superstitions　　c. misunderstandings

10) In our culture, snails are not considered valiant animals — we are constantly **exhorting** people to "come out of their shells" — but there's a lot to be said for taking your home with you wherever you go.

a. persuading　　b. asking　　c. warning

Reading

The Power of Introverts: A Manifesto for Quiet Brilliance

1 Do you enjoy having time to yourself, but always feel a little guilty about it? Then Susan Cain's "Quiet: The Power of Introverts" is for you. It's part book, part manifesto. We live in a nation that values its **extroverts** — the outgoing, the lovers of crowds — but not the quiet types who change the world. She recently answered questions from Mind Matters editor Gareth Cook.

2 **Cook: This may be a stupid question, but how do you define an introvert? How can somebody tell whether they are truly introverted or extroverted?**

Cain: Not a stupid question at all! **Introverts** prefer quiet, minimally stimulating environments, while extroverts need higher levels of stimulation to feel their best. Stimulation comes in all forms — social stimulation, but also lights, noise, and so on. Introverts even salivate more than extroverts do if you place a drop of lemon juice on their tongues! So an introvert is more likely to enjoy a quiet glass of wine with a close friend than a loud, raucous party full of strangers.

It's also important to understand that introversion is different from shyness. Shyness is the fear of negative judgment, while introversion is simply the preference for less stimulation. Shyness is **inherently** uncomfortable; introversion is not. The traits do overlap, though psychologists debate to what degree.

3 **Cook: You argue that our culture has an extroversion bias. Can you explain what you mean?**

Cain: In our society, the ideal self is bold, gregarious, and comfortable in the spotlight. We like to think that we value individuality, but mostly we admire the type of individual who's comfortable "putting himself out there." Our schools, workplaces, and religious institutions are designed for extroverts. Introverts are to extroverts what American women were to men in the 1950s — second-class citizens with gigantic amounts of untapped talent.

In my book, I travel the country — from a Tony Robbins seminar to Harvard Business School to Rick Warren's powerful Saddleback Church — **shining a light on** the bias against introversion. One of the most poignant moments was when an evangelical pastor I met at Saddleback confided his shame that "God is not pleased" with him because he likes spending time alone.

4 **Cook: How does this cultural inclination affect introverts?**

Cain: Many introverts feel there's something wrong with them, and try to pass as extroverts. But whenever you try to pass as something you're not, you lose a part of yourself along the way. You especially lose a sense of how to spend your time. Introverts are constantly going to parties and such when they'd really prefer to be home reading, studying, inventing, **meditating**, designing, thinking, cooking…or any number of other quiet and worthwhile activities.

According to the latest research, one third to one half of us are introverts — that's one out of every two or three people you know. But you'd never guess that, right? That's because introverts learn from an early age to act like pretend-extroverts.

5 Cook: Is this just a problem for introverts, or do you feel it hurts the country as a whole?

Cain: It's never a good idea to organize society in a way that **depletes** the energy of half the population. We discovered this with women decades ago, and now it's time to realize it with introverts. This also leads to a lot of wrongheaded notions that affect introverts and extroverts alike. Here's just one example: Most schools and workplaces now organize workers and students into groups, believing that creativity and productivity comes from a gregarious place. This is nonsense, of course. From Darwin to Picasso to Dr. Seuss,* our greatest thinkers have often worked in solitude, and in my book I examine lots of research on the **pitfalls** of groupwork.

6 Cook: Tell me more about these "pitfalls of groupwork."

Cain: When you're working in a group, it's hard to know what you truly think. We're such social animals that we **instinctively** mimic others' opinions, often without realizing we're doing it. And when we do disagree consciously, we pay a psychic price. The Emory University neuroscientist Gregory Berns found that people who dissent from group wisdom show heightened activation in the amygdala, a small organ in the brain associated with the sting of social rejection. Berns calls this the "pain of independence." Take the example of brainstorming sessions, which have been wildly popular in corporate America since the 1950s, when they were pioneered by a charismatic ad executive named Alex Osborn. Forty years of research shows that brainstorming in groups is a terrible way to produce creative ideas. The organizational psychologist Adrian Furnham puts it pretty bluntly: The "evidence from science suggests that business people must be insane to use brainstorming groups. If you have talented and motivated people, they should be encouraged to work alone when creativity or efficiency is the highest priority." This is not to say that we should abolish groupwork. But we should use it a lot more judiciously than we do today.

7 Cook: What are some of the other misconceptions about introverts and extroverts?

Cain: One big one is the notion that introverts can't be good leaders. According to groundbreaking new research by Adam Grant, a management professor at Wharton, introverted leaders sometimes deliver better outcomes than extroverts do. Introverts are more likely to let talented employees run with their ideas, rather than trying to put their own stamp on things. And they tend to be motivated not by ego or a desire for the spotlight, but by dedication to their larger goal. The ranks of transformative leaders in history illustrate this: Gandhi, Eleanor Roosevelt, and Rosa Parks were all introverts, and so are many of today's business leaders, from Douglas Conant of Campbell Soup to Larry Page at Google.

8 Cook: Is there any relationship between introversion and creativity?

Cain: Yes. An interesting line of research by the psychologists Mihaly Csikszentmihalyi and Gregory Feist suggests that the most creative people in many fields are usually introverts. This is probably because introverts are comfortable spending time alone, and solitude is a crucial (and underrated) ingredient for creativity.

9 Cook: Can you give some other examples of surprising introversion research?

Cain: The most surprising and fascinating thing I learned is that there are "introverts" and "extroverts" throughout the animal kingdom – all the way down to the level of fruit flies! Evolutionary biologist David Sloan Wilson speculates that the two types evolved to use very different survival strategies. Animal "introverts" stick to the sidelines and survive when predators come calling. Animal "extroverts" roam and explore, so they do better when food is scarce. The same is true (analogously speaking) of humans.

10 Cook: Are you an introvert?

Cain: Yes. People sometimes seem surprised when I say this, because I'm a pretty friendly person. This is one of the greatest **misconceptions** about introversion. We are not anti-social; we're *differently* social. I can't live without my family and close friends, but I also crave solitude. I feel incredibly lucky that my work as a writer affords me hours a day alone with my laptop. I also have a lot of other introvert characteristics, like thinking before I speak, disliking conflict, and concentrating easily.

Introversion has its annoying qualities, too, of course. For example, I've never given a speech without being terrified first, even though I've given many. (Some introverts are perfectly comfortable with public speaking, but stage fright afflicts us in disproportionate numbers.)

But I also believe that introversion is my greatest strength. I have such a strong inner life that I'm never bored and only occasionally lonely. No matter what mayhem is happening around me, I know I can always turn inward.

In our culture, snails are not considered valiant animals – we are constantly **exhorting** people to "come out of their shells" — but there's a lot to be said for taking your home with you wherever you go.

*Note

Dr. Seuss: U.S. author of children's books, such as *The Cat in the Hat* and *Fox in Socks*

Part 2 Understanding the Reading

Answer the following questions. Then compare your answers with classmates.

1. How does Susan Cain define "introverts" and "extroverts"?

2. According to Cain, how is "shyness" different from introversion?

3. What do you think Cain means by saying that "our culture has an extroversion bias"?

4. Susan Cain says, "Introverts are to extroverts what American women were to men in the 1950s — second-class citizens with gigantic amounts of untapped talent." (paragraph 3) What does she mean by this sentence? How are introverts compared to American women in the 1950s? What is the similarity between them?

5. How does Cain explain "the pitfalls of groupwork"? What do you think we should beware of when we use group work?

6. What does the following phrase mean: "put their own stamp on things" (paragraph 7)?

7. What does Cain think about the relationship between introversion and creativity?

8. Cain concludes the interview by saying that "In our culture, snails are not considered valiant animals — we are constantly exhorting people to "come out of their shells" — but there's a lot to be said for taking your home with you wherever you go." (paragraph 10) What does she mean? What is the overall message Susan Cain wants to convey?

Part 3 Getting the Main Idea

1. To make sure that you understand the passage, take notes about the main idea and the main points.

2. Compare your notes with your group members.

Part 4 Personalizing

1. Cain says, "Our schools, workplaces, and religious institutions are designed for extroverts." Do you agree with her idea? Why or why not? If you think so, how do you think they are designed for extroverts, for example?

____

____

____

____

2. Do you have any personal experiences of feeling uneasy or uncomfortable because you are an introvert or an extrovert?

____

____

____

____

____

Part 5 Sharing

Share your opinion with your group members about the author's viewpoint. Did you find any interesting ideas from your classmates? What are they? What do you think?

Part 6 Critical Thinking & Reflection

It's reflection time!

1. Discuss with group members similarities and differences you have found through sharing ideas. In discussion, did you come across any new points of view?

2. Have you changed your idea after getting to know your classmates' opinions? Why or why not?

Part 7 Expressing Your Ideas

Write down your own opinion about the theme of this reading, "the importance of solitude." Use your notes to explain your thinking to your group members.

____

____

____

____

____

____

Choose one of the following tasks.

1. OPINION WRITING

Write your ideas about the theme of this unit, "How can you contribute to making a better society?" Illustrate your ideas with examples from the readings in this textbook or from your own ideas.

2. GROUP PROJECT

Group work and individual work have their own advantages and disadvantages. Considering these advantages and disadvantages, think about what kind of task will be suitable for group work or individual work. Give some reasons to support your opinion. After discussing, give a short presentation to the class.

Language & Communication

UNIT THREE

Rawpixel.com/Shutterstock

Theme

What is most important for communication between people in our culture and outside?

Reading 1 A Linguistic Big Bang (By Lawrence Osborne) *The New York Times Magazine* (1999/10/24)

Reading 2 Could the Lingua Franca Approach to Learning Break Japan's English Curse? (By Kris Kosaka) *The Japan Times* (2014/08/17)

Reading 3 Love That Lingua Franca. Trip Talk: Travel Encounters Can Benefit From a Common Third Language (By Daisann McLane) *National Geographic Traveler* (September 2016)

A Linguistic Big Bang

Part 1 Warm-up

1. Pre-reading Questions

Think about the following questions and share your ideas with classmates.

1. What do you think "A Linguistic Big Bang" refers to? Predict the content of the reading passage from its title.
2. How would you communicate with someone whose language you had no knowledge of at all?
3. Do you know anything about sign languages? Do you think they are just like spoken languages having their own complex systems of grammar and vast amounts of vocabulary?

2. Vocabulary Check

Guess the meaning of the bold-faced words from the context and choose the best one.

1) Not being **privy** to the more than 200 existing sign languages used by hearing-impaired people around the world, Managua's deaf children started from ground zero.

   a. knowing about b. finding interesting c. paying attention to

2) They had no grammar or syntax—only crude gestural signs developed within their own families. These **pantomimes**, which deaf kids use to communicate basic needs like "eat," "drink" and "ice cream," are called *mimicas* in Spanish.

   a. dramas with no words b. written figures c. heavy breathing

3) Steven Pinker, author of "The Language Instinct," sees what happened in Managua as proof that language acquisition is **hard-wired** inside the human brain.

   a. difficult to learn b. suspended c. genetically determined

4) We've been able to see how it is that children — not adults — generate language, and we have been able to record it happening in great scientific detail. And it's the first and only time that we've actually seen a language being created **out of thin air**.

   a. from precious resources b. apparently from nowhere c. insubstantially

UNIT THREE

5) Indeed, the Managua teachers say they left hardly an imprint on the children's **improvised** language—largely because their lack of experience led them to adopt poor pedagogy.

a. created from available resources   b. new   c. clumsy

6) Because the students had no **prior** concept of words (let alone letters), it proved fruitless to try to communicate in this fashion.

a. primary   b. sophisticated   c. already existing

7) It was noticeable at once that the younger children used signs in a more **nuanced** way than the older students.

a. subtle   b. innovative   c. educated

8) … this apparently small difference had enormous **implications**.

a. conclusions that can be drawn   b. influences   c. reasons for their existence

9) … an original group of home signers **came up with** an elemental pidgin among themselves

a. arrived   b. created   c. gave each other

10) "Real language in this case," she says, "only **emerged** with young children first exposed to a signed pidgin."

a. became stronger   b. became acceptable   c. developed

Reading

A Linguistic Big Bang

1 For the first time in history, scholars are witnessing the birth of a language—a complex sign system being created by deaf children in Nicaragua—which proves a linguistic theory that grammar is biological rather than cultural.

2 Following the 1979 Sandinista revolution, the newly installed Nicaraguan Government inaugurated the country's first large-scale effort to educate deaf children. Hundreds of students were enrolled in two Managua schools. Not being **privy** to the more than 200 existing sign languages used by hearing-impaired people around the world, Managua's deaf children started from ground zero. They had no grammar or syntax—only crude gestural signs developed within their own families. These **pantomimes**, which deaf kids use to communicate basic needs like "eat," "drink" and "ice cream," are called *mimicas* in Spanish.

3 Most of the children arrived in Managua with only a limited repertory of *mimicas*. But once the students were placed together, they began to build on one another's signs. One child's gesture solidified into the community's word. The children's inexperienced teachers—who were having paltry success communicating with their profoundly deaf students—watched in awe as the kids began signing among themselves. A new language had begun to bloom.

4 A decade later, the children's creation has become a sensation of modern linguistics. Nicaraguan Sign Language (known to experts as I.S.N., for *Idioma de Signos Nicaragense*) has been patiently decoded by outside scholars, who describe an idiom filled with curiosities yet governed by the same "universal grammar" that the linguist Noam Chomsky[*1] claims structures all language. Steven Pinker[*2], author of "The Language Instinct," sees what happened in Managua as proof that language acquisition is **hard-wired** inside the human brain. "The Nicaraguan case is absolutely unique in history," he maintains. "We've been able to see how it is that children—not adults—generate language, and we have been able to record it happening in great scientific detail. And it's the first and only time that we've actually seen a language being created **out of thin air**."

5 Managua's deaf children were stranded in school, not on a desert island. Spanish-speaking teachers were there to guide them. Yet it turns out that Nicaraguan Sign Language doesn't resemble Spanish at all. Indeed, the Managua teachers say they left hardly an imprint on the children's **improvised** language—largely because their lack of experience led them to adopt poor pedagogy. When the schools first opened, the Sandinista education officials were misguidedly urged by Soviet advisers to adopt "finger spelling" which uses simple signs to limn the alphabets of spoken languages. This approach was a disaster. Because

the students had no **prior** concept of words (let alone letters), it proved fruitless to try to communicate in this fashion. The children remained linguistically disconnected from their teachers.

6 This failure to adopt a workable teaching strategy, paradoxically, gave the Nicaraguan children an opportunity to erect a linguistic structure of their own. Indeed, the frustrated Managua teachers began to notice that although the children could barely communicate with their instructors, they were beginning to communicate well among themselves, using a sign system that no teacher recognized. But what, exactly, was it?

7 In June 1986, the Nicaraguan Ministry of Education contacted Judy Kegl, an American sign-language expert at Northeastern University. They invited her to visit the deaf schools in Managua and see if she could shed some light on the enigma. Armed with notebooks and a Pentax camera—and a vague tenderness for the revolution—the 33-year-old Kegl set off for Managua.

8 Her first stop was Villa Libertad, a vocational school for deaf teenagers. Kegl, now a professor at the University of Southern Maine in Portland, set out to make a rudimentary dictionary of the signs being used by a small group of adolescent girls in a hairdressing workshop. Some signs were obvious enough: objects like "eyebrow tweezers" and "rolling curlers" were signed by more or less imitating the things themselves. But one day, a student playfully tested a more intricate sign on her. She first laid out her left palm flat; then, using her right hand, she traced a line from the middle finger to the base of the palm, turning her right hand over afterward and pointing below her belt. As a result of the girl's giggling, Kegl guessed that the sign meant "sanitary napkin." She had learned her first word in what seemed to be a simple form of communication.

9 After a few days, Kegl figured out the sign for "house" and could combine it with a typical Nicaraguan gesture for "What's up?"—a strong wrinkle of the nose—to ask the deaf students where they lived. The students' responses, however, were baffling. Each student would produce a series of complex but apparently meaningless hand wriggles. Only later would Kegl figure out that these wriggles were in fact precise descriptions of Managua's labyrinthine bus routes. Indeed, the grammar underlying this enigmatic sign system completely eluded her. "I felt like I was failing as a linguist," she recalls. "I couldn't find any consistent regularities. It seemed to be complete chaos."

10 Three weeks later, however, Kegl moved on to the primary school, known as San Judas, where younger children were being taught. On the first day, she observed a young girl named Mayela Rivas signing in a courtyard. Her gestures were rapid and had an eerie rhythmic consistency. Kegl sensed that Mayela was not just making crude *mimicas* or the kind of signed pidgin practiced by the older students at Villa Libertad.

11 "I looked at her, and I thought to myself, Holy cow, that girl is using some kind of rule book," she says. Ann Senghas, a former assistant of Kegl's who is now a professor at Barnard College, shares her wonder. "It was a linguist's dream," she says. "It was like being present at the Big Bang."

12 It was noticeable at once that the younger children used signs in a more **nuanced** way than the older students. For example, the teenage pidgin signers at Villa Libertad had a basic gesture for "speak"—*opening* and *closing* four fingers and a thumb in front of the mouth. The younger children used the same sign, but modulated it, opening their fingers at the position of the speaker and closing them at the position of the addressee. To Kegl, this apparently small difference had enormous **implications**. "This was verb agreement," she says, "and they were all using it fluently." Similarly, the younger kids could express what linguists call "spatial agreement" with their verbs. When they used the verb "to fall"—as in "Mr. Koumal falls down the mountain"—they made a link between Mr. Koumal's falling and what he was falling down. These nuanced signers would first lift one hand in the air to signify "mountaintop" and then begin the sign for "fall" from this height, flipping the hand back and forth while moving it down an imaginary slope.

13 What explained this difference between the younger and older signers? Kegl's theory, which has been disseminated in various linguistic journals, is that an original group of home signers **came up with** an elemental pidgin among themselves. This was the comparatively crude signing she had observed among the older students. Then, very young children of 5 or 6 had come into the school system. Quickly mastering the pidgin from their elder peers, they had then taken it, quite unconsciously, to a far higher level. This second version was the fast, elegantly orchestrated language that Kegl had seen flying from the little fingers of Mayela Rivas. This was what would become known as the *idioma*, or Nicaraguan Sign Language. These three quite distinct levels—home signs, the pidgin and the sign language—represent phases of evolution, from pantomime to pidgin to language. "Real language in this case," she says, "only **emerged** with young children first exposed to a signed pidgin."

*Notes

1 Noam Chomsky: a famous U.S. linguist whose theory of Universal Grammar assumes that grammar is an innate capacity of humans

2 Steven Pinker: U.S. linguist and author of *The Language Instinct*, which supports Chomsky's theory of Universal Grammar

Part 2 Understanding the Reading

Answer the following questions. Then compare your answers with classmates.

1. The writer mentions "a linguistic theory that grammar is biological rather than cultural." (paragraph 1) What does the writer mean by the word "biological"?

2. What did the Nicaraguan Government do in 1979?

3. What happened when deaf children were placed together in Managua schools?

4. Why does the writer think the "finger spelling" approach failed? (paragraph 7)

5. What does Judy Kegl mean by "I felt like I was failing as a linguist"? (paragraph 11) Why do you think she mentions this?

6. What did Judy Kegl notice when she was observing young children at the primary school called San Judas?

7. What does the writer mean by "spatial agreement"? (paragraph 12) Note that "verb agreement" refers to the grammatical phenomenon of a verb changing its form according to the grammatical features of a concomitant noun, usually a subject noun (e.g. I know …, She knows …).

8. According to Kegl's theory, there are three stages the development of Nicaraguan Sign Language has gone through. What are each of the stages called? How does she describe each stage? Complete the following chart to understand Kegl's theory:

The 1st Stage: mimicas/pantomimes
- Simple gestural signs developed and used within each deaf child's family.
- Having no (   ), with only a limited (   ).

↓

The 2nd Stage : (   )
- A crude signing or simple form of communication shared by teenagers.

↓

The 3rd Stage : the sign language/ Nicaraguan Sign Language
- A real language developed by very young children of 5 or 6 who were exposed to (   ).
- Having their own intricate system of grammar (e.g. spatial agreement)

Part 3 Getting the Main Idea

1. To make sure that you understand the passage, take notes about the main idea and the main points.

2. Compare your notes with your group members.

Part 4 Personalizing

1. This article describes how Nicaraguan deaf children created their own language without knowledge of any language in order to communicate among themselves. Have you ever tried to communicate with someone whose language you did not know?

2. Have you ever made up a language or a code that you used only with one other person or a small group of friends?

Part 5 Sharing

Share your opinion with your group members about the author's viewpoint. Did you find any interesting ideas from your classmates? What are they? What do you think?

Part 6 Critical Thinking & Reflection

It's reflection time!

1. Discuss with group members similarities and differences you have found through sharing ideas. In discussion, did you come across any new points of view?

2. Have you changed your idea after getting to know your classmates' opinions? Why or why not?

Part 7 Expressing Your Ideas

Write down your own opinion about the theme of this reading, "Grammar is innate, not only a learned phenomenon." Use your notes to explain your thinking to your group members.

____

____

____

____

____

____

Reading 2

Could the Lingua Franca Approach to Learning Break Japan's English Curse?

Part 1 Warm-up

1. Pre-reading Questions

Think about the following questions and share your ideas with classmates.

1. What language skills do you want to acquire or improve?
2. Do you think it is necessary to try to speak English like a native speaker?

2. Vocabulary Check

Guess the meaning of the bold-faced words from the context and choose the best one.

1) "Japanese people sometimes **hesitate** to speak English, but in reality we do not need to reach native level, with perfect English, in order to communicate," argues Nakamura.

   a. are quick　　b. are reluctant　　c. are keen

2) To communicate is the most important thing, so we need to **get rid of** this barrier, especially in the workplace.

   a. eradicate　　b. climb　　c. avoid

3) A current global trend in language learning could help: the teaching of English as a **lingua franca** (ELF).

   a. foreign language　　b. common language　　c. native language

4) Unlike the similar-looking **acronym** EFL (English as a foreign language), which targets native-level fluency, ELF involves approaching the language as a common tongue between non-native speakers.

   a. nickname　　b. proper name　　c. name taken from initial letters

5) **Advocates** of English as a lingua franca are open to models of non-native English, such as Singlish (Singapore English) and variations of Indian English, which emphasize communication over grammatical perfection and stress the importance of building relationships, …

   a. critics　　b. speakers　　c. proponents

6) Non-native speakers far **outnumber** native English speakers around the world.

   a. are less than　　b. are more than　　c. are the same as

7) I think it's fair to say Japan has not **interfaced** well with globalization and …

a. connected with   b. looked toward   c. transformed

8) Living abroad and having that experience to live **immersed** in a different perspective is an invaluable experience.

a. rejected by   b. unused to   c. surrounded by

Reading

Could the Lingua Franca Approach to Learning Break Japan's English Curse?

1 According to EF Education First's English Proficiency Index, English ability among Japanese is flat-lining—and may even be falling—"despite enormous private investment."

2 In a damning assessment, EF concludes that "In the past six years, Japanese adults have not improved their English. If anything, their skills have declined slightly. During the same period, other Asian countries, most notably Indonesia and Vietnam, have made enormous progress. Despite being a far wealthier and more developed country, Japan is struggling to teach its students English for use in a competitive global economy."

3 Newspaper headlines constantly speak of tweaks and reforms to English education here, yet school lessons remain teacher-centered and grammar-heavy, with much of the instruction conducted in Japanese. This means "students have no opportunity to practice or apply new skills," EF says, meaning many Japanese lack confidence when it comes to speaking English despite spending years learning the language.

4 "Since the ranking is always a comparison to other countries, it indicates that other Asian countries have changed their education system," explains EF Japan President Junnosuke Nakamura. "In Japan, we have not actually changed anything at a fundamental level. For example, the Tokyo Metropolitan Government recently sent their English teachers abroad to try and improve their level of English, and it is a first step. But too often in our schools, a Japanese national is teaching English in Japanese, and English must be taught in English. So we really need to change the fundamental way of teaching at the earliest level.

5 "Japanese people sometimes **hesitate** to speak English, but in reality we do not need to reach native level, with perfect English, in order to communicate," argues Nakamura. "To communicate is the most important thing, so we need to **get rid of** this barrier, especially in the workplace. Trying to communicate, trying to say what you think — not speaking perfect English — that is important."

6 A current global trend in language learning could help: the teaching of English as a **lingua franca** (ELF). Unlike the similar-looking **acronym** EFL (English as a foreign language), which targets native-level fluency, ELF involves approaching the language as a common tongue between non-native speakers. Literally meaning "Frankish tongue," lingua franca originally referred to the mixture of Italian, French, Greek, Arabic, and Spanish used in Mediterranean trade for centuries. Much more recently, and particularly in Europe, the ELF approach has become increasingly popular among linguists and teachers of English, who see the idea as a natural fit for the increasingly globalized world we live in.

7 **Advocates** of English as a lingua franca are open to models of non-native English, such as Singlish (Singapore English) and variations of Indian English, emphasize communication over grammatical perfection, and stress the importance of building relationships, accommodating the other speaker's language level and working toward shared understanding. In the classroom, English is taught with specific communication goals in mind rather than with grammatical drills, even allowing for non-standard grammatical patterns, provided communication is achieved.

8 Mike Handford, a professor of linguistics at the University of Tokyo, welcomes this global shift toward accepting a variety of English standards. "In terms of past research into language and language teaching, the native speaker is the model and the idea is to become like a native speaker for success as a second language learner," he says. "But the reality is, it is virtually impossible to become like a native speaker in another language. By setting up the native speaker as the only model, you are setting up your students to fail."

9 Non-native speakers far **outnumber** native English speakers around the world. According to the British Council, over 750 million people use English as a foreign language compared to only 375 million people who speak it as their first language. With at least 75 countries listing English as a "special status" language, ELF opens up the linguistic floodgates to a torrent of English from a wide range of international sources.

10 "If Japan could become aware of different communication techniques, using English as a lingua franca for more functional purposes, that makes a lot of sense," says linguist Paul Cunningham of Rikkyo University. "I think it's fair to say Japan has not **interfaced** well with globalization and is really missing out on what globalization has to offer."

11 Both professors admit there are still many hurdles to overcome before teaching English as a lingua franca takes off in Japan. A quick scroll through popular job listing sites for English teachers in Japan reveals an almost universal demand for native speakers, but Handford relates how his daughter's current assistant language teacher at her public elementary school in Fujisawa, Kanagawa Prefecture, is Filipino—something he believes "10 years ago would have been unusual, but now is more common with the acceptance of a variety of English models."

12 Communication involves more than language skills, Handford argues: Flexibility and interpersonal skills are equally as important.

"The way that somebody talks to their parents about what happened at school is completely different to the way they will talk to their friends, and it is not only vocabulary — it's body language, it's attitude; in some ways they become different people. Once students are made aware of their multiple identities in communication, it is easier to transfer that idea to language."

13 "There has been a greater recognition around the world that native monolingual speakers are often not very good in international situations—another reason they may not be the ideal language model for communication." For example, "American or British monolingual teachers may lack empathy or the skill sets of trying to communicate in a second language," Handford says. "A good English speaker using it as a second language in a lingua franca tradition may be much better at these kinds of interpersonal skills, making accommodations for their listener's language level, empathizing with someone whose language skills may not be high."

14 For the Japanese business world to truly accept the ELF model, all aspects of intercultural communication must be taught, Handford says—including the development of multiple identities in work situations.

15 "Japan has historically emphasized or exaggerated its cultural differences, the cultural uniqueness of Japan. It causes problems for Japanese speakers of another language, as they immediately feel the differences, and this can hamper communication," Handford argues. "Developing a more dynamic notion of identity, realizing there are far more similarities across cultures than differences—to encourage learners to appreciate this can be quite empowering. By making students aware of their multiple identities when using other languages, it allows them to behave differently in appropriate situations more consciously and strategically."

16 Cunningham believes the best way for anyone to develop an idea of multiple identities for intercultural communication is by traveling outside their home countries. A requirement in Rikkyo's Intercultural Communication Department, where Cunningham works, is that every student spends one full semester overseas.

"Living abroad and having that experience to live **immersed** in a different perspective is an invaluable experience," says Cunningham. "It's not all about language. By looking at the world through a different lens, students can build off that experience to become more receptive to different contexts and situations, and that is an accomplishment towards intercultural communication."

Part 2 Understanding the Reading

Answer the following questions. Then compare your answers with classmates.

1. What does EF conclude from the results of EF Education First's English Proficiency Index?

2. What does EF think are the problems with English education in Japan?

3. What does ELF stand for? How is it different from the EFL approach?

4. Mike Handford says, "By setting up the native speaker as the only model, you are setting up your students to fail." (paragraph 8) What does he mean by this sentence?

5. What does Handford think about the ELF approach? Why does he think so?

6. What does Mike Handford mean by "multiple identities"? (paragraph 12)

7. What do Mike Handford and Paul Cunningham think is necessary for the EFL approach to successfully achieve its goal?

Part 3 Getting the Main Idea

1. To make sure that you understand the passage, take notes about the main idea and the main points.

2. Compare your notes with your group members.

Part 4 Personalizing

1. This article argues that thinking of English as a lingua franca would be a better approach for Japanese English education. How did you learn English when you were a junior and senior high school student? Would you say the approach to English at your school was EFL or ELF?

____

____

____

____

2. How would you like to improve your English communication ability? How could you create or increase opportunities to communicate with other people in English?

____

____

____

____

____

Part 5 Sharing

Share your opinion with your group members about the author's viewpoint. Did you find any interesting ideas from your classmates? What are they? What do you think?

Part 6 Critical Thinking & Reflection

It's reflection time!

1. Discuss with group members similarities and differences you have found through sharing ideas. In discussion, did you come across any new points of view?

2. Have you changed your idea after getting to know your classmates' opinions? Why or why not?

Part 7 Expressing Your Ideas

Write down your own opinion about the theme of this reading, "Thinking of English as a lingua franca could improve English education in Japan." Use your notes to explain your thinking to your group members.

____

____

____

____

____

Reading 3

Love That Lingua Franca. Trip Talk: Travel Encounters Can Benefit From a Common Third Language

Part 1 Warm-up

1. Pre-reading Questions

Think about the following questions and share your ideas with classmates.

1. Have you experienced memorable encounters during your travels to other places? Who did you meet? Why was it so memorable?
2. How do you feel when you talk in English with someone whose native language is English?
3. Do you have any experiences of talking in English with someone whose native language is neither English nor your native language? If so, how did you feel then? If not, do you think you would feel different from when you talk in English with a native speaker of English?

2. Vocabulary Check

Guess the meaning of the bold-faced words from the context and choose the best one.

1) In such situations I often use my camera for show-and-tell but it's **running out of battery juice**.

   a. broken　　b. water-damaged　　c. the battery is nearly out of power

2) So I **resign myself** to a couple of hours filled with stilted, polite English.

   a. dislike　　b. accept the situation　　c. give up

3) A basic knowledge of at least one other language is a handy item to have in your travel tool kit, for it **levels** the playing field.

   a. makes both sides equal　　b. destroys all obstacles　　c. Raises your ability

4) Thanks to the worldwide **penetration** of the English language, usually when I travel I'm talking to people from another culture and language who are straining to speak mine.

   a. spread　　b. domination　　c. teaching

5) …I'm talking to people from another culture and language who are **straining** to speak mine.

   a. making an unusually great effort　　b. moving in one direction

c. moving away aimlessly from the right place

6) Since I believe every traveler should speak other languages, I have spent years learning two myself, Spanish and Cantonese. This introduces the flip side of the travel-language **dilemma**.

a. ability b. pronunciation c. difficult situation

7) The not-native-to-either-party language is like a **neutral** territory, a halfway point where the joys and difficulties of communication are shared equally.

a. not belonging to either side b. colourless c. peaceful

8) So I grab every chance I get to use that most democratic and **liberating** language of all, the third tongue.

a. political b. loose c. freeing

9) I greeted them with an "*¡Hola!*" and we **ended up** having lunch together.

a. before we parted b. as a result c. finished our conversation

10) Was that Cantonese **drifting** from the group of people next to me on the street? I listened more closely.

a. pouring out b. partially audible c. dropped

Reading

Love That Lingua Franca.
Trip Talk: Travel Encounters Can Benefit From a Common Third Language

1 Michiko, the young Japanese woman I'm sharing a seat with on a bus near Tokyo, speaks a shy, hesitant English. In such situations I often use my camera for show-and-tell, but it's **running out of battery juice**. So I **resign myself to** a couple of hours filled with stilted, polite English. "What country are you from? Do you like our Japanese sushi?" But then something unexpected happens. Grasping for a subject to talk about with her, I spot the headline on the cover of a local tourism leaflet, written in Japanese and English. Japanese has Chinese characters in its writing system and I can read Chinese, so I immediately notice that the characters for the Japanese word "Chiba" mean "One Thousand Leaves." How perfect, I think, looking out the bus window at a rich autumn panorama of golden gingko and flame-red maple trees blanketing the hillsides.

2 Pointing to the leaflet, I turn to Michiko and say: "Chiba means one thousand leaves." She perks up. "Yes!" she responds, then adds in a French accent that is way better than mine, "*Milles feuilles*."

"*Mais alors*," I say, "*vous parlez français?*"

No, she answers, and, once again in a pitch-perfect accent, says "*Hablo español*."

Fantastic! "*Yo también* — me too," I tell her. We've found common ground, and race into an extended conversation. As shy as Michiko is in English, she's confident, funny, and even a bit saucy when she speaks in Spanish.

3 It has been observed that we often change personalities when we switch languages. I don't speak any Japanese, so I don't know what Michiko is like in her mother tongue. In the third tongue of Spanish, however, we blast past not just linguistic but cultural differences to have a real—and soon a dishy, even intimate—conversation. "*¿Te gustan los hombres latinos?*" she asks me. Do I like Latin men?

4 This isn't the first time I've experienced the thrill of connecting on the road with someone in a third-party tongue, which is what I call a common language that's non-native to both speakers. A basic knowledge of at least one other language is a handy item to have in your travel tool kit, for it **levels** the playing field.

5 Thanks to the worldwide **penetration** of the English language, usually when I travel I'm talking to people from another culture and language who are **straining** to speak mine. While I never take this effort for granted, and I certainly appreciate it, having the linguistic advantage makes me feel impolite somehow. And guilty, because I'm never going to spend years mastering Tamil or Thai or Japanese.

6 Since I believe every traveler should speak other languages, I have spent years learning two myself, Spanish and Cantonese. This introduces the flip side of the travel-language **dilemma**. When I'm in Madrid or Guangzhou (formerly known as Canton), I do my best to keep pace with the rapid-fire, slangy conversation of native speakers who always seem to be tossing around vocabulary words that weren't in my study books. I lean forward into the conversations and listen with all my concentration and heart, but after a while of struggling I become exhausted and frustrated, and soon give up.

7 The not-native-to-either-party language is like a **neutral** territory, a halfway point where the joys and difficulties of communication are shared equally. I speak more slowly, knowing that my listeners may not "hear" me like a native; they return the favor. We all leave out tricky turns of phrase.

8 The late English novelist Angela Carter, who spent some years living in Japan in the 1970s, wrote, "Language is power, life, and the instrument of culture, the instrument of domination and liberation." As a traveler, I want my words to bring me closer to people, not pound them over the head with the reminder that my language is on the global A-list of linguae francae. So I grab every chance I get to use that most democratic and **liberating** language of all, the third tongue.

9 Sometimes just finding a third tongue can be an adventure. One day in India's northern state of Rajasthan, I wandered through a Jain temple, mostly not noticing the murmur of voices in Hindi—or was it Gujarati?—around me, when my ear latched on to a very familiar rhythm of sounds. I turned and found four European women discussing the architectural details of the temple in lispy castellano Spanish. I greeted them with an "*¡Hola!*" and we **ended up** having lunch together. Because they had so tired of speaking in their third tongue, English, as they made their way around English-speaking India, they were happy to slow down their native Spanish for me.

10 Then there was the time in Shanghai when I lost my way as I wandered the streets outside the Yu Yuan Garden, in the city's Old Town. Mandarin, the official language of mainland China, is the dominant language here, making the Cantonese I'd learned in Hong Kong not very useful. Night was falling, and no taxi would stop to pick me up. Just then, my ear clutched at something. Was that Cantonese **drifting** from the group of people next to me on the street? I listened more closely. No, darn, it was Mandarin. Still, with desperation setting in, I went over to them anyway and asked in Cantonese if they knew where the taxi stand was.

11 To my surprise, one of the young men answered in "my" Chinese.
"I am from Shanghai, so my first language is Shanghainese," he explained. "I also speak Mandarin, of course. But now I work in a factory in the city of Guangzhou, so I learned Cantonese there."

12 He then strode right into the traffic-filled street and practically dragged a taxi back with him. As I thanked him, a thought hit me: In China, with its multiple languages and dialects, people communicate in third tongues all the time. Maybe someday the whole world will.

13 Back in the bus with Michiko, we finally pull up to our destination, an old Shinto temple perching on top of a mountain. The classic Japanese setting exerts the powerful force of place, pulling Michiko and me away from our lingua franca detour to Madrid and its *hombres latinos* and placing us squarely in the present. We fall out of Spanish and back into our mother languages and our roles: the local person and the foreign tourist. Now, though, we know the third tongue will be there when we need it.

Part 2 Understanding the Reading

Answer the following questions. Then compare your answers with classmates.

1. What was the conversation between the writer and Michiko like when they were talking in English?

2. What made a change in their conversation? How did it change?

3. The writer says, "A basic knowledge of at least one other language is a handy item to have in your travel kit, for it levels the playing field"? (paragraph 4) What does she mean by saying that "it levels the playing field"?

4. The writer mentions "the travel-language" dilemma. (paragraph 6) What does the dilemma refer to?

5. The writer says, "The not-native-to-either-party language is like a neutral territory." (paragraph 7) What does she mean by "not-native-to-either-party language" and "like a neutral territory"?

6. The writer describes the third language as "the most democratic and liberating language of all" (paragraph 8) What does she mean by this phrase? In what sense is it democratic and liberating?

7. What is the writer's purpose in introducing the three experiences she had in Japan, India, and Shanghai?

8. What is the overall message the author would like to convey?

Part 3 Getting the Main Idea

1. To make sure that you understand the passage, take notes about the main idea and the main points.

2. Compare your notes with your group members.

Part 4 Personalizing

1. This article shows that in intercultural communication, there are advantages to using a language that is not native to either speaker. What do you think matters most in communication for the writer? Do you agree with her ideas? Why or why not?

____

____

____

____

2. Do you think travelers should learn the native languages of the countries or communities they will visit? Why or why not?

____

____

____

____

____

Part 5 Sharing

Share your opinion with your group members about the author's viewpoint. Did you find any interesting ideas from your classmates? What are they? What do you think?

Part 6 Critical Thinking & Reflection

It's reflection time!

1. Discuss with group members similarities and differences you have found through sharing ideas. In discussion, did you come across any new points of view?

2. Have you changed your idea after getting to know your classmates' opinions? Why or why not?

Part 7 Expressing Your Ideas

Write down your own opinion about the theme of this reading, "Using a third language to speak to people from other countries." Use your notes to explain your thinking to your group members.

____

____

____

____

____

____

Choose one of the following tasks.

1. OPINION WRITING

What are some of the problems of communication between people of different cultures and what do you think is the best way to solve them? Illustrate your ideas with examples from the readings in this textbook or from your own research.

2. GROUP PROJECT

Reading 2 in this unit focuses on some advantages of the lingua franca approach to English education. Think about potential problems with the approach and some possible solutions to them. Discuss in a small group and give a short presentation to the class.

Learning & Emotion

UNIT FOUR

bleakstar/Shutterstock

Theme

How does "emotion" affect learning?

Reading 1 To Help Students Learn, Engage the Emotion (by Jessica Lahey) *The New York Times* (2016/05/04)

Reading 2 The Effort Effect (by Marina Krakovsky) Cover story of March/April 2007 *Stanford Magazine* (March/April 2007)

Reading 3 The Dark Side of Emotional Intelligence (by Adam Grant) *The Atlantic* (2014/01/02)

Reading 1

To Help Students Learn, Engage the Emotion

Part 1 Warm-up

1. Pre-reading Questions

Think about the following questions and share your ideas with classmates.

1. How do you feel when you are learning something new?
2. What kind of learning do you feel is boring?
3. When do you get interested in learning and want to know much more?

2. Vocabulary Check

Guess the meaning of the bold-faced words from the context and choose the best one.

1) During a period of significant racial and ethnic tension at the school, she struggled to engage her students in a unit on human **evolution**.

   a. transfer of power　　b. gradual development　　c. overthrow of social order

2) She understands the reason behind her students' shift from **apathy** to engagement and, finally, to deep, meaningful learning.

   a. lack of interest　　b. clearly understanding　　c. hope of achieving something

3) After days of apathy and **outright** resistance to Ms. Immordino-Yang's teaching, a student finally asked the question that altered her teaching.

   a. extremely angry　　b. external　　c. open and direct

4) Dr. Immordino-Yang's eyes light up as she **recounts** this story in her office.

   a. tells someone about something　　b. returns to a normal state of health
   c. takes into account

5) While she'd provided me with pages of quotes, studies and images meant to illustrate all she wanted to teach me during those two hours in her office, her enthusiasm for the topic served as the most powerful **exhibit**.

   a. breathing out　　b. a public display of works of art
   c. a document or other object produced as evidence

6) The best, most **durable** learning happens when content sparks interest, when it is relevant to a child's life, and when the students form an emotional bond with either the subject at hand or the teacher.

a. consisting of two parts　　b. long-lasting　　c. throughout the course

7) Creating this emotional connection can be a **daunting** task.

a. seeming difficult to deal with　　b. not easy to satisfy　　c. not interesting

8) Research has shown that the investment reaps huge **dividends** in the form of increased learning and better grades.

a. amount　　b. a part of profit that is divided among members　　c. successes

9) The girl dreamed of becoming a dairy farmer like her father and grandfather, and felt that her classes were **irrelevant**.

a. not balanced　　b. different from each other　　c. not connected with each other

Reading

To Help Students Learn, Engage the Emotion

1 Before she became a neuroscientist, Mary Helen Immordino-Yang was a seventh-grade science teacher at a school outside Boston. One year, during a period of significant racial and ethnic tension at the school, she struggled to engage her students in a unit on human **evolution**. After days of apathy and **outright** resistance to Ms. Immordino-Yang's teaching, a student finally asked the question that altered her teaching—and her career path—forever: "Why are early hominids always shown with dark skin?"

2 With that question, one that connected the abstract concepts of human evolution and the very concrete, personal experiences of racial tension in the school, her students' resistance gave way to interest. As she explained the connection between the effects of equatorial sunlight, melanin and skin color and went on to explain how evolutionary change and geography result in various human characteristics, interest blossomed into engagement, and something magical happened: Her students began to learn.

3 Dr. Immordino-Yang's eyes light up as she **recounts** this story in her office at the Brain and Creativity Institute at the University of Southern California. Now an associate professor of education, psychology and neuroscience, she understands the reason behind her students' shift from **apathy** to engagement and, finally, to deep, meaningful learning.

Her students learned because they became emotionally engaged in material that had personal relevance to them.

4 Emotion is essential to learning, Dr. Immordino-Yang said, and should not be underestimated or misunderstood as a trend, or as merely the "E" in "SEL," or social-emotional learning. Emotion is where learning begins, or, as is often the case, where it ends. Put simply, "It is literally neurobiologically impossible to think deeply about things that you don't care about," she said.

This rule holds true even across subjects and disciplines, Dr. Immordino-Yang writes in her book, "*Emotions, Learning, and the Brain.*" "Even in academic subjects that are traditionally considered unemotional, such as physics, engineering or math, deep understanding depends on making emotional connections between concepts."

5 As a teacher, I know what an emotionally engaged student looks like on the outside, but Dr. Immordino-Yang showed me what that student looks like on the inside using a functional M.R.I., a scanner that reveals brain function in real time.

"When students are emotionally engaged," she said, "we see activations all around the cortex*[1], in regions involved in cognition, memory and meaning-making, and even all the way down into the brain stem."

As she went on to explain why emotion is vital to high-quality learning, Ms. Immordino-Yang's cheeks flushed pink, her eyes brightened, and her hands became animated and expressive. While she'd provided me with pages of quotes, studies and images meant to illustrate all she wanted to teach me during those two hours in her office, her enthusiasm for the topic served as the most powerful **exhibit**.

6 Great teachers understand that the best, most **durable** learning happens when content sparks interest, when it is relevant to a child's life, and when the students form an emotional bond with either the subject at hand or the teacher in front of them. Meaningful learning happens when teachers are able to create an emotional connection to what might otherwise remain abstract concepts, ideas or skills.

Creating this emotional connection might sound like a **daunting** task, but research has shown that the investment reaps huge **dividends** in the form of increased learning and better grades. When teachers take the time to learn about their students' likes, dislikes and personal interests, whether it's racial issues brewing at their school, their after-school job, or their dreams and goals, learning improves.

7 I experienced this a few years ago, with a parent who asked me how to get her daughter interested in school. The girl dreamed of becoming a dairy farmer like her father and grandfather, and felt that her classes were **irrelevant**.

And yet, given a few moments to think and some creativity, we both realized that dairy farming is a perfect laboratory for everything from biology to math, chemistry to geometry, history to government; all of these subjects are relevant and important in the life of a dairy farmer. When the catalog for I.V.F.-ready bull semen arrives in the mail, she'll need to know about dominant and recessive genetic traits. She'll need to understand soil chemistry, microbiology, botany, the geometry of herd rotation as it relates to land use, and the political and financial realities of keeping dairy farming viable as an industry.

8 The emotional connection that can result when teachers make learning personally relevant to students is what differentiates superficial, rote, topical assimilation of material from a superlative education marked by deep mastery and durable learning. While there are no silver bullets in education, emotional engagement and personal relevance is the tool that has the potential to improve the educational experience of every child, in every school in America.

*Note: cortex: the tissue forming the outer layer of an organ or structure in animals

Part 2 Understanding the Reading

Answer the following questions. Then compare your answers with classmates.

1. Why do you think her students' resistance gave way to interest?

2. What does the following phrase mean: "they (students) became emotionally engaged in material"? (paragraph 3)

3. The author says, "Emotion is essential to learning." (paragraph 4) Why does she think so?

4. Why does the author describe Ms. Immordino-Yang's expression in detail? (paragraph 5)

5. When do the best, most durable learning and meaningful learning happen?

6. Why does the author tell us the story of one of her students who wanted to be a dairy farmer?

7. What is the most effective way to enable learners to learn deeply?

Part 3 Getting the Main Idea

1. To make sure that you understand the passage, take notes about the main idea and the main points.

2. Compare your notes with your group members.

Part 4 Personalization

1. The author suggests that "emotional engagement and personal relevance" are essential for real learning. Do you agree with her viewpoint? Why or why not?

____

____

____

____

2. Do you have any experience or do you know any examples which support your point of view? What are they?

____

____

____

____

____

Part 5 Sharing

Share your opinion with your group members about the author's viewpoint. Did you find any interesting ideas from your classmates? What are they? What do you think?

Part 6 Critical Thinking & Reflection

It's reflection time!

1. Discuss with group members similarities and differences you have found through sharing ideas. In discussion, did you come across any new points of view?

2. Have you changed your idea after getting to know your classmates' opinions? Why or why not?

Part 7 Expressing Your Ideas

Write down your own opinion about the theme of this reading, "Emotional engagement is essential to learn deeply." Use your notes to explain your thinking to your group members.

____

____

____

____

____

____

Reading 2
The Effort Effect

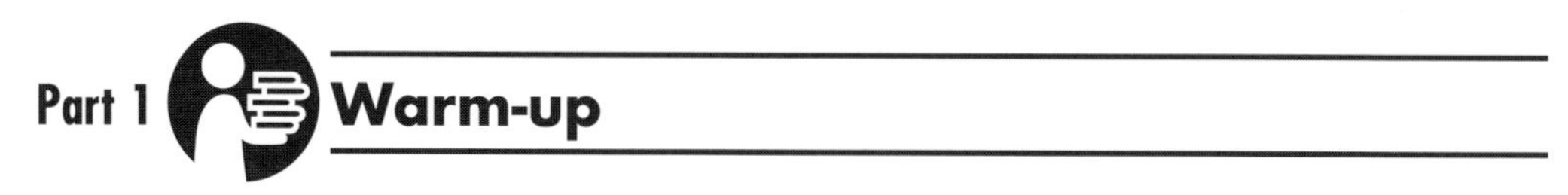

1. Pre-reading Questions

Think about the following questions and share your ideas with classmates.

1) Which do you think is necessary to become a successful athlete, hard practice or natural talent?
2) How do you feel when you fail?
3) Do you think ability can be developed?

2. Vocabulary Check

Guess the closest synonyms of the words in parenthesis and choose the best one from the list.

chalked up,	immense,	zest,	setbacks,	inherent

1) Despite suffering three terrible (difficulties or problems), he succeeded in becoming an Olympic athlete. ____________
2) I've got a(n) (extremely large) capacity for work. ____________
3) She had a great (enjoyment and enthusiasm) for life. ____________
4) He (considered that something is caused by something) his success to effort. ____________
5) There are risks (being a basic part of something) in almost every business. ____________

posited,	surmounted,	paramount,	disdained

6) Dweck (suggested something is true) that the difference between the helpless response and the determination to master new things lay in people's beliefs about why they had failed. ____________
7) She was well aware of the difficulties that had to be (overcome) . ____________
8) For some students performance is (more important than anything else). ____________
9) Ignoring the team's motto—"skill and hard work"—the most talented individuals (considered to be unworthy) serious training. ______________

Reading

The Effort Effect

1 One day last November, psychology professor Carol Dweck welcomed a pair of visitors from the Blackburn Rovers, a soccer team in the United Kingdom's Premier League. The Rovers' training academy is ranked in England's top three, yet performance director Tony Faulkner had long suspected that many promising players weren't reaching their potential. Ignoring the team's century-old motto—*arte et labore*, or "skill and hard work"—the most talented individuals **disdained** serious training.

2 On some level, Faulkner knew the source of the trouble: British soccer culture held that star players are born, not made. If you buy into that view, and are told you've got **immense** talent, what's the point of practice? If anything, training hard would tell you and others that you're merely good, not great. Faulkner had identified the problem; but to fix it, he needed Dweck's help.

3 A 60-year-old academic psychologist might seem an unlikely sports motivation guru. But Dweck's expertise—and her recent book, *Mindset: The New Psychology of Success*—bear directly on the sort of problem facing the Rovers. Through more than three decades of systematic research, she has been figuring out answers to why some people achieve their potential while equally talented others don't—why some become Muhammad Ali and others Mike Tyson. The key, she found, isn't ability; it's whether you look at ability as something **inherent** that needs to be demonstrated or as something that can be developed.

4 What's more, Dweck has shown that people can learn to adopt the latter belief and make dramatic strides in performance. These days, she's sought out wherever motivation and achievement matter, from education and parenting to business management and personal development.

5 As a graduate student at Yale, Dweck started off studying animal motivation. In the late 1960s, a hot topic in animal research was "learned helplessness": lab animals sometimes didn't do what they were capable of because they'd given up from repeat failures. Dweck wondered how humans coped with that. "I asked, 'What makes a really capable child give up in the face of failure, where other children may be motivated by the failure?'" she recalls.

6 At the time, the suggested cure for learned helplessness was a long string of successes. Dweck **posited** that the difference between the helpless response and its opposite—the determination to master new things and **surmount** challenges—lay in people's beliefs about why they had failed. People who attributed their failures to lack of ability, Dweck thought, would become discouraged even in areas where they were capable. Those who

thought they simply hadn't tried hard enough, on the other hand, would be fueled by **setbacks**. This became the topic of her PhD dissertation.

7 Dweck and her assistants ran an experiment on elementary school children whom school personnel had identified as helpless. These kids fit the definition perfectly: if they came across a few math problems they couldn't solve, for example, they no longer could do problems they had solved before—and some didn't recover that ability for days.

8 Through a series of exercises, the experimenters trained half the students to **chalk up** their errors to insufficient effort, and encouraged them to keep going. Those children learned to persist in the face of failure—and to succeed. The control group showed no improvement at all, continuing to fall apart quickly and to recover slowly. These findings, says Dweck, "really supported the idea that the attributions were a key ingredient driving the helpless and mastery-oriented patterns." Her 1975 article on the topic has become one of the most widely cited in contemporary psychology.

9 Attribution theory, concerned with people's judgments about the causes of events and behavior, already was an active area of psychological research. But the focus at the time was on how we make attributions, explains Stanford psychology professor Lee Ross, who coined the term "fundamental attribution error" for our tendency to explain other people's actions by their character traits, overlooking the power of circumstances. Dweck, he says, helped "shift the emphasis from attributional errors and biases to the consequences of attributions—why it matters what attributions people make." Dweck had put attribution theory to practical use.

10 She continued to do so as an assistant professor at the University of Illinois, collaborating with then-graduate student Carol Diener to have children "think out loud" as they faced problem-solving tasks, some too difficult for them. The big surprise: some of the children who put forth lots of effort didn't make attributions at all. These children didn't think they were failing. Diener puts it this way: "Failure is information—we label it failure, but it's more like, 'This didn't work, I'm a problem solver, and I'll try something else.'" During one unforgettable moment, one boy—something of a poster child for the mastery-oriented type—faced his first stumper by pulling up his chair, rubbing his hands together, smacking his lips and announcing, "I love a challenge."

11 Such **zest** for challenge helped explain why other capable students thought they lacked ability just because they'd hit a setback. Common sense suggests that ability inspires self-confidence. And it does for a while—so long as the going is easy. But setbacks change everything. Dweck realized—and, with colleague Elaine Elliott soon demonstrated—that the difference lay in the kids' goals. "The mastery-oriented children are really hell-bent on learning something," Dweck says, and "learning goals" inspire a different chain of thoughts and behaviors than "performance goals."

12 Students for whom performance is **paramount** want to look smart even if it means not learning a thing in the process. For them, each task is a challenge to their self-image, and each setback becomes a personal threat. So they pursue only activities at which they're sure to shine—and avoid the sorts of experiences necessary to grow and flourish in any endeavor. Students with learning goals, on the other hand, take necessary risks and don't worry about failure because each mistake becomes a chance to learn. Dweck's insight launched a new field of educational psychology—achievement goal theory.

Part 2 Understanding the Reading

Answer the following questions. Then compare your answers with classmates.

1. What was the trouble with the Blackburn Rovers, a soccer team in the United Kingdom's Premier League?

2. What is the result of the belief that "star players are born, not made"?

3. How do children who have "learned helplessness" react to failure?

4. How can helpless students overcome the helpless response?

5. What did Carol prove by the experiment conducted with elementary school children?

6. During an experiment with elementary school children, Carol Diener experienced one unforgettable moment. What was that?

7. According to Dweck, what is the difference between "learning goals" and "performance goals"? Explain in your own words.

8. In what point is "achievement goal theory" new to psychologists?

Part 3 Getting the Main Idea

1. To make sure that you understand the passage, take notes about the main idea and the main points.

2. Compare your notes with your group members.

Part 4 Personalization

1. Do you agree with Dweck's "achievement goal theory"? Why or why not?

____

____

____

____

2. Which type are you, mastery-oriented or learning-oriented? Why do you think so?

____

____

____

____

____

Part 5 Sharing

Share your opinion with your group members about the author's viewpoint. Did you find any interesting ideas from classmates? What are they? What do you think?

Part 6 Critical Thinking & Reflection

It's reflection time!

1. Discuss with group members similarities and differences you have found through sharing ideas. In discussion, did you come across any new points of view?

2. Have you changed your idea after getting to know your classmates' opinions? Why or why not?

Part 7 Expressing Your Ideas

Write down your own opinion about the theme of this reading, "Effort is much more important than ability." Why do you think so? Use your notes to explain your thinking to your group members.

Reading 3

The Dark Side of Emotional Intelligence

Part 1 Warm-up

1. Pre-reading Questions

Think about the following questions and share your ideas with classmates.

1. Can an ability to motivate others be used for unethical purposes?
2. Do you think that our emotions can hinder our ability to think rationally?
3. Do you think that emotional intelligence is a necessary skill in the workplace?

2. Vocabulary Check

Guess the meaning of the bold-faced words from the context and choose the best one.

1) Martin Luther King Jr's ability to deliver such an **electrifying** message required emotional intelligence—the ability to recognize, understand, and manage emotions.

   a. enlightening   b. powerful and impressive   c. fatal

2) One of the most influential leaders of the 20th century spent years studying the emotional effects of his body language, which allowed him to become an absolutely **spellbinding** public speaker.

   a. hypnotic   b. complex   c. expert

3) Emotional intelligence has been **touted** by leaders, policymakers, and educators as the solution to a wide range of social problems.

   a. mistaken   b. explained   c. promoted, sold

4) According to experts, emotional intelligence helps people **disguise** one set of emotions while expressing another for personal gain.

   a. reject   b. conceal, mask   c. display

5) When people hone their emotional skills, they become better at **manipulating** others.

   a. attracting   b. controlling   c. impressing

6) When a leader gave an inspiring speech filled with emotion, the audience was less likely to **scrutinize** the message.

   a. listen to   b. admire   c. examine

7) Emotionally intelligent people intentionally shape their emotions to **fabricate** favorable impressions of themselves.

a. make   b. believe   c. choose

8) Emotional intelligence was **consequential** when examining certain behaviors.

a. predictable   b. relevant   c. unimportant

9) When colleagues were treated unjustly, they felt the **righteous** indignation to speak up.

a. correct   b. direct   c. justified

10) When employees **went out on a limb** to advocate for gender equity, emotional intelligence helped them keep their fear at bay.

a. took a risk   b. raised their hands   c. left their company

Reading

The Dark Side of Emotional Intelligence

1 Some of the greatest moments in human history were fueled by emotional intelligence. When Martin Luther King, Jr. presented his dream, he chose language that would stir the hearts of his audience. "Instead of honoring this sacred obligation" to liberty, King thundered, "America has given the Negro people a bad check." He promised that a land "sweltering with the heat of oppression" could be "transformed into an oasis of freedom and justice," and envisioned a future in which "on the red hills of Georgia sons of former slaves and the sons of former slave-owners will be able to sit down together at the table of brotherhood."

2 Delivering this **electrifying** message required emotional intelligence—the ability to recognize, understand, and manage emotions. Dr. King demonstrated remarkable skill in managing his own emotions and in sparking emotions that moved his audience to action. As his speechwriter Clarence Jones reflected, King delivered "a perfectly balanced outcry of reason and emotion, of anger and hope. His tone of pained indignation matched that note for note."

3 Recognizing the power of emotions, another one of the most influential leaders of the 20th century spent years studying the emotional effects of his body language. Practicing his hand gestures and analyzing images of his movements allowed him to become "an absolutely **spellbinding** public speaker," says the historian Roger Moorhouse—"it was something he worked very hard on." His name was Adolf Hitler.

4 Since the 1995 publication of Daniel Goleman's bestseller, emotional intelligence has been **touted** by leaders, policymakers, and educators as the solution to a wide range of social problems. If we can teach our children to manage emotions, the argument goes, we'll have less bullying and more cooperation. If we can cultivate emotional intelligence among leaders and doctors, we'll have more caring workplaces and more compassionate healthcare. As a result, emotional intelligence is now taught widely in secondary schools, business schools, and medical schools.

5 Emotional intelligence is important, but the unbridled enthusiasm has obscured a dark side. New evidence shows that when people hone their emotional skills, they become better at **manipulating** others. When you're good at controlling your own emotions, you can disguise your true feelings. When you know what others are feeling, you can tug at their heartstrings and motivate them to act against their own best interests.

6 Social scientists have begun to document this dark side of emotional intelligence. In emerging research led by University of Cambridge professor Jochen Menges, when a

leader gave an inspiring speech filled with emotion, the audience was less likely to **scrutinize** the message and remembered less of the content. Ironically, audience members were so moved by the speech that they claimed to recall more of it.

7 The authors call this the awestruck effect, but it might just as easily be described as the dumbstruck effect. One observer reflected that Hitler's persuasive impact came from his ability to strategically express emotions—he would "tear open his heart"—and these emotions affected his followers to the point that they would "stop thinking critically and just emote."

8 Leaders who master emotions can rob us of our capacities to reason. If their values are out of step with our own, the results can be devastating. New evidence suggests that when people have self-serving motives, emotional intelligence becomes a weapon for manipulating others. In a study led by the University of Toronto psychologist Stéphane Côté, university employees filled out a survey about their Machiavellian tendencies, and took a test measuring their knowledge about effective strategies for managing emotions. Then, Coté's team assessed how often the employees deliberately undermined their colleagues. The employees who engaged in the most harmful behaviors were Machiavellians with high emotional intelligence. They used their emotional skills to demean and embarrass their peers for personal gain.

9 Shining a light on this dark side of emotional intelligence is one mission of a research team led by University College London professor Martin Kilduff. According to these experts, emotional intelligence helps people **disguise** one set of emotions while expressing another for personal gain. Emotionally intelligent people "intentionally shape their emotions to **fabricate** favorable impressions of themselves," Professor Kilduff's team writes. "The strategic disguise of one's own emotions and the manipulation of others' emotions for strategic ends are behaviors evident not only on Shakespeare's stage but also in the offices and corridors where power and influence are traded."

10 Of course, people aren't always using emotional intelligence with evil intents. More often than not, emotional skills are simply instrumental tools for goal accomplishment. In a study of emotions at the Body Shop, a research team led by Stanford professor Joanne Martin discovered that founder Anita Roddick leveraged emotions to inspire her employees to fundraise for charity. As Roddick explained, "Whenever we wanted to persuade our staff to support a particular project we always tried to break their hearts." However, Roddick also encouraged employees to be strategic in the timing of their emotion expressions. In one case, after noticing that an employee often "breaks down in tears with frustration," Roddick said it was acceptable to cry, but "I told her it has to be used. I said, 'Here, cry at this point in the ... meeting.'" When viewing Roddick as an exemplar of an emotionally intelligent leader, it becomes clear that there's a fine line between motivation and manipulation. Walking that tightrope is no easy task.

11 In settings where emotions aren't running high, emotional intelligence may have hidden costs. Recently, psychologists Dana Joseph of the University of Central Florida and Daniel Newman of the University of Illinois comprehensively analyzed every study that has ever examined the link between emotional intelligence and job performance. Across hundreds of studies of thousands of employees in 191 different jobs, emotional intelligence wasn't consistently linked with better performance. In jobs that required extensive attention to emotions, higher emotional intelligence translated into better performance. Salespeople, real-estate agents, call-center representatives, and counselors all excelled at their jobs when they knew how to read and regulate emotions—they were able to deal more effectively with stressful situations and provide service with a smile.

12 However, in jobs that involved fewer emotional demands, the results reversed. The more emotionally intelligent employees were, the *lower* their job performance. For mechanics, scientists, and accountants, emotional intelligence was a liability rather than an asset. Although more research is needed to interpret these results, one promising explanation is that these employees were paying attention to emotions when they should have been focusing on their tasks. If your job is to analyze data or repair cars, it can be quite distracting to read the facial expressions, vocal tones, and body languages of the people around you. In suggesting that emotional intelligence is critical in the workplace, perhaps we've put the cart before the horse.

13 Instead of assuming that emotional intelligence is always useful, we need to think more carefully about where and when it matters. In a recent study at a healthcare company, I asked employees to complete a test about managing and regulating emotions, and then asked managers to evaluate how much time employees spent helping their colleagues and customers. There was no relationship whatsoever between emotional intelligence and helping: Helping is driven by our motivations and values, not by our abilities to understand and manage emotions. However, emotional intelligence was **consequential** when examining a different behavior: challenging the status quo by speaking up with ideas and suggestions for improvement.

14 Emotionally intelligent employees spoke up more often and more effectively. When colleagues were treated unjustly, they felt the **righteous** indignation to speak up, but were able to keep their anger in check and reason with their colleagues. When they **went out on a limb** to advocate for gender equity, emotional intelligence helped them keep their fear at bay. When they brought ideas for innovation to senior leaders, their ability to express enthusiasm helped them avoid threatening leaders. On a much smaller scale, they were able to follow Martin Luther King Jr.'s lead in rocking the boat while keeping it steady.

15 There is growing recognition that emotional intelligence—like any skill—can be used for good or evil. So if we're going to teach emotional intelligence in schools and develop it at work, we need to consider the values that go along with it and where it's actually useful. As Professor Kilduff and colleagues put it, it is high time that emotional intelligence is "pried away from its association with desirable moral qualities."

Part 2 Understanding the Reading

Answer the following questions. Then compare your answers with classmates.

1. What special skill did Martin Luther King Jr. and Adolf Hitler have in common?

2. What is "the dark side" of emotional intelligence?

3. Why does the author believe that teaching emotional intelligence in schools and workplaces is not sufficient?

4. What did the proponents of Daniel Goleman's concept believe would be the benefits of teaching emotional intelligence in secondary schools, business schools, and medical schools?

5. What is meant by the expression "to tug at (one's) heartstrings"?

6. What tendency did Jochen Menges and his team discover in audiences of speeches that were filled with emotional content?

7. What is meant by "Machiavellian tendencies"? How did the subjects with Machiavellian tendencies and high emotional intelligence in Stéphane Côté's study tend to behave toward their colleagues?

8. What is meant by the following: "There's a fine line between motivation and manipulation. Walking that tightrope is no easy task"? How was this illustrated in Anita Roddick's example?

9. How is helping others different from emotional intelligence?

Part 3 Getting the Main Idea

1. To make sure that you understand the passage, take notes about the main idea and the main points.

2. Compare your notes with your group members.

Part 4 Personalization

1. Do you feel you have emotional intelligence?
   How important do you think it is for you now or in the future?

____

____

____

____

2. In what situations do you imagine you would need to be emotionally intelligent, or aware of the emotional intelligence of other people?

____

____

____

____

____

Part 5 Sharing

Share your opinion with your group members about the author's viewpoint. Did you find any interesting ideas from your classmates? What are they? What do you think?

Part 6 Critical Thinking & Reflection

It's reflection time!

1. Discuss with group members similarities and differences you have found through sharing ideas. In discussion, did you come across any new points of view?

2. Have you changed your idea after getting to know your classmates' opinions? Why or why not?

Part 7 Expressing Your Ideas

Write down your own opinion about the theme of this reading, "EI can block reason and morality." Why do you think so? Use your notes to explain your thinking to your group members.

____

____

____

____

____

____

Choose one of the following tasks.

1. OPINION WRITING

Write your opinion on the theme of this unit, "Learning and Emotion."
How do you motivate yourselves to achieve your goals? Illustrate your ideas with examples from the readings in this textbook or from your own research.

2. GROUP PROJECT

1) Search for a famous inspiring speech. Why do you think it is successful at inspiring (motivating?) others? Discuss with your group members. Give a short presentation with your group members. Don't forget to show the speech you chose.

2) Watch the following TED talk by Simon Sinek and discuss his theory of the Golden Circle. Working in your group, find other examples of successful companies or leaders that do (or do not) follow the Golden Circle model and present your findings to the class.
https://www.ted.com/talks/simon_sinek_how_great_leaders_inspire_action

Useful Phrases and Vocabulary for Effective Writing

APPENDIX

1. REPORTING VERBS

When you want to report or summarize what someone else wrote, many verbs can be used in the expressions: [Person][verb] that ....; or As [person][verb], ...

Some verbs put more emphasis on the original author's beliefs and are often used if you want to show that your own opinion is different.

Verbs	Examples
argue	The minister argued that, as our society is ageing, the only way to reduce the tax burden on working people is to increase immigration.
believe	Many people believe that video games are harmful to young children.
claim	In a new study, researchers claim that young people require more than 8 hours sleep every night.
suggest	In her latest book, the famous psychologist suggests that our mind set determines whether we will be successful or not.
think	Education researchers now think that teachers should cater to children's different learning styles.

Other verbs put more emphasis on the information that is reported, and these are useful if you want to agree with what the original author says.

Verbs	Examples
mention	In a television interview, the president mentioned that he had initially decided not to stand for re-election but had subsequently changed his mind.
note	As the interviewer noted, the president had never spoken in public about his decision to run for office before.
point out	The president then pointed out that he had never been asked about this before.
say	The interviewer said that he was grateful to the president for revealing his true feelings to the television viewers.

2. TRANSITION SIGNALS

When you want to clearly show how one idea is related to another idea, you can use the following transition signals.

1) Clarifying Information/Terminology	
In other words,	The people who are most likely to succeed are those with a positive mindset, in other words, those who see the reason for past failure as behaviors that they can change
To put it simply,	Chomsky introduced a theory of Universal Grammar. To put it simply, grammar is something we are born with.
That is,	I want to meet you where we met last time, that is, outside the school gate by the big tree.
2) Giving Reasons	
One/Another/A third reason (for …) is …	In recent years, fewer university students have opted to study abroad. One reason for this is the pressure of job hunting.
This is because …	Many students today do not own a dictionary. This is because they can access dictionaries on their smart phones.
This is due to …	The weather will be unusually warm this weekend. This is due to a warm front approaching from the south.
3) Giving Examples	
For example/instance,	There are many activities you can do at home for practicing English, for instance, listening to music while reading the lyrics, or watching a movie while reading the subtitles.
(More) specifically,	The summer months in Japan are hot and humid. More specifically, July and August can be very uncomfortable.
…, such as …	I am a fan of classical music composers, such as Mozart and Beethoven.
4) Expressing Similarities	
Similarly (Likewise), …	The UK is an island nation. Similarly (Likewise), Japan is a country that has no land borders with other countries.
Like …,	Like Japan, the UK's nominal head of state is a monarch.
Just as …,	Just as Japan has four seasons, in the UK, spring, summer, autumn and winter are different and beautiful in their own ways.

5) Expressing Differences	
However, …	Many people believe that breakfast is the most important meal of the day. However, I believe that a relaxing evening meal is essential for health and well-being.
On (the) one hand/ On the other hand, …	I cannot decide which jacket to buy. On (the) one hand, the blue one is very fashionable. On the other hand, the black one is more practical for work.
On the contrary, …	My father doesn't dislike sweets. On the contrary, he eats more than is good for him.
In contrast to …,	My father loves sweets, in contrast to my mother who never eats sugar at all.
Unlike …,	My father eats sweets every day, unlike my mother, who never eats them at all.
While/whereas …	My father eats sweets every day, while my mother never eats them at all.

WEBSITES

Unit 1

Reading 1 http://www.japantimes.co.jp/news/2009/10/11/national/science-health/in-cross-cultural-situations-remember-those-emoticons/#.WYA4vojyg2x

Reading 2 https://www.japantimes.co.jp/opinion/2017/12/16/commentary/world-commentary/nurture-important-nature-success/#.W6uLMvZuLZ4

Reading 3 https://www.jahonline.org/article/S1054-139X(17)30355-5/fulltext

October 2017 Volume 61, Issue 4, Supplement

http://dx.doi.org/10.1016/j.jadohealth.2017.07.009

Unit 2

Reading 1 https://www.theatlantic.com/business/archive/2015/01/the-secret-to-smart-groups -isnt-smart-people/384625/

Reading 2 https://www.japantimes.co.jp/news/2015/09/15/national/social-issues/japanese-firms-need-diverse-workforce-says-harvard-academic/#.W6roEPZuJPY

Reading 3 https://www.scientificamerican.com/article/the-power-of-introverts/

Unit 3

Reading 1 http://www.nytimes.com/library/magazine/home/19991024mag-sign-language.html

Reading 2 http://www.japantimes.co.jp/community/2014/08/17/issues/could-the-lingua-franca-approach-to-learning-break-japans-english-curse/#.WYA7m4jyg2w

Reading 3 http://travel.nationalgeographic.com/travel/traveler-magazine/real-travel/language/

Unit 4

Reading 1 https://well.blogs.nytimes.com/2016/05/04/to-help-students-learn-engage-the -emotions/?_r=0

Reading 2 http://marinakrakovsky.com/the-effort-effect-stanford-marchapril-2007/

Reading 3 https://www.theatlantic.com/health/archive/2014/01/the-dark-side-of -emotional-intelligence/282720/

TED talk by Simon Sinek:
https://www.ted.com/talks/simon_sinek_how_great_leaders_inspire_action

■ 監修者：著者（執筆順）紹介

氏名：舘岡　洋子（たておか　ようこ）

担当：監修

現職：早稲田大学大学院日本語教育研究科教授

最終学歴：早稲田大学大学院教育学研究科
博士（学術）

主な著書：『ピア・ラーニング入門―創造的な学びのデザインのために』（ひつじ書房、2007、共著）
『日本語教育のための質的研究入門』（ココ出版、2015、編著、第1章）

氏名：津田　ひろみ（つだ　ひろみ）

担当：「はじめに」、Unit 4

現職：明治大学国際日本学部非常勤講師、他

最終学歴：立教大学大学院異文化コミュニケーション研究科
博士（異文化コミュニケーション学）

主な著書・論文：『学習者の自律をめざす協働学習―中学校英語授業における実践と分析』（ひつじ書房、2013）
「大学授業における協働学習の効果の検証―自律的な学習者の育成を目指して」『明治大学教職課程年報―別府昭郎先生退職記念号』38号（明治大学、2016）

氏名：Alison Stewart（アリスン・スチュアート）

担当：「Getting Started」、Unit 3

現職：学習院大学英語英米文化学科教授

最終学歴：University of London
博士（Applied Linguistics）

主な著書・論文：「Realizing autonomy: Contradictions in practice and context」『*Realizing autonomy: Practice and reflection in language education contexts*』（Basingstoke: Palgrave Macmillan、2012、編著、Chapter 1）
「Clarifying terms」『*Collaborative learning in learner development*』（JALT Publications、2014、編著、Chapter 1）(eBook)

氏名：大須賀　直子（おおすか　なおこ）

担当：Unit 1

現職：明治大学国際日本学部教授

最終学歴：ランカスター大学大学院
博士（言語学）

主な著書：「The speech act of complaint performed by Japanese EFL learners: A pilot study」『*Global Japanese Studies Review*』No.6（明治大学、2014）
「Development of pragmatic routines by Japanese learners in a study abroad context」『*Current Issues in Intercultural Pragmatics*』（John Benjamins、2017、Chapter 12）

氏名：小松　千明（こまつ　ちあき）

担当：Unit 2

現職：お茶の水女子大学文教育学部非常勤講師、他

最終学歴：お茶の水女子大学大学院
博士（人文科学）

主な著書：『アルファ英文法』（研究社、2010年、共著、1章、4章～11章、15章、22章）

Critical Reading through Collaborative Learning

Supervised by Tateoka Yoko

Tsuda Hiromi, Osuka Naoko, Komatsu Chiaki, Alison Stewart

発行	2019年3月29日　初版1刷
定価	2200円＋税
監修者	舘岡洋子
著者	津田ひろみ・大須賀直子・小松千明・Alison Stewart
発行者	松本功
装丁者	杉枝友香（asahi edigraphy）
本文組版者	星谷陽子（asahi edigraphy）
印刷・製本所	株式会社 シナノ
発行所	株式会社 ひつじ書房

〒112-0011 東京都文京区千石2-1-2 大和ビル2階
Tel.03-5319-4916 Fax.03-5319-4917
郵便振替 00120-8-142852
toiawase@hituzi.co.jp　http://www.hituzi.co.jp/

ISBN978-4-89476-930-4